Fast & Fun
Mental Math

250 Quick Quizzes to Sharpen Math Skills
Every Day of the School Year

By Chuck Lotta

SCHOLASTIC
PROFESSIONAL BOOKS

New York • Toronto • London • Auckland • Sydney
Mexico City • New Delhi • Hong Kong

Dedication

This book is dedicated to the teachers who have faithfully used its methods over the years. Kudos to the math teachers at Barrett Middle School in San Juan Unified School District, Sacramento, California, who recognized the need for it and suggested ideas. I also salute the hundreds of enthusiastic student teachers at Chapman University, Sacramento Campus, who continue to spread mental math skills wherever they teach.

—Chuck Lotta

Cover design by Jaime Lucero and Norma Ortiz
Cover art by Alfred Schrier

Interior design by Drew Hires
Interior illustrations by Drew Hires

ISBN: 0-439-13848-5

Table of Contents

Introduction

FAST & FUN MENTAL MATH provides you with an enjoyable, nonthreatening, and effective way to help students memorize important math vocabulary, ideas, symbols, and operations. After using the quizzes in this resource, your students will do much better on regular math textbook work and end-of-year tests, and easily apply their skills to real-life math problems. They will approach math problems with much greater confidence.

FAST & FUN MENTAL MATH can be presented as a warm-up activity, a nonthreatening test at the beginning or end of a formal math lesson, or when you have an extra ten minutes anytime during the school day. Students get out their weekly answer sheet (which has different mental math tips each week) and try to answer ten questions or problems read aloud by the teacher. They must figure the answers in their heads, not on paper. The teacher repeats each question two to three times during a 20-second span, then moves to the next question so the students are clearly demonstrating instant recall or mental calculation. At the end of the ten questions (about three minutes), each student swaps papers with a partner and marks the answers with either a "C" for correct answers or an "X" if they're wrong. The correct answers are then entered on the Monday results line.

During the correction time, the teacher takes time to teach or explain any vocabulary word, procedure, or concept that gave students difficulty. This is the most powerful part of the method because the students will pay close attention to these mini-lessons when you tell them they will be hearing these questions probably next week and again throughout the year.

After Friday's set of questions is corrected, the total number of correct answers for the week is entered in the week's total box. The papers are then returned to their owners, and the addition is double-checked.

Students who score high or show dramatic improvement from previous quizzes might be awarded math bonus points or funny stickers to put on their binders, like football players get on their helmets for making good plays. Everyone wins! The incentive is personal . . . for each student to learn and remember as much as possible throughout the year.

This method deliberately introduces new and old vocabulary and concepts students should know, but haven't been taught, haven't mastered, or have forgotten. Almost all of the students will soon know how to round off and estimate numbers; know the properties of geometric figures; know how to square numbers and find square roots; understand positive and negative integers; relate fractions, decimal numbers, and percentages; and be introduced to algebraic equations.

Another way to use this book is to provide students with photocopies of the quizzes so students practice visual mental math. Tell them they have to solve the problems in their heads, not on scratch paper. Students who have difficulty visualizing the oral problems might do better when the problems are in front of them on paper. When they finish, they swap papers and go through the 50 questions as if it were a Friday. The teacher can once again explain difficult problems on the board. Doing this every two weeks will help them reinforce their mental math abilities.

How to Use This Book

There are 50 weeks of questions in this book. The difficulty of the questions are such that an average 4th-grade class would go from Week 1 to Week 20, an average 5th-grade class from Week 10 to Week 30, an average 6th-grade class from Week 20 to Week 40, and 7th-and 8th-grade classes would go from Week 30 to 50. However, since classes vary in math aptitude and experience, some 5th-, 6th-, or 7th-grade classes might start several weeks earlier than the weeks recommended above, and some 4th-, 5th-, or 6th-grade classes might start several weeks beyond the recommended starting week—you be the judge! You want both success and growth. FAST & FUN MENTAL MATH works well with 3/4, 4/5, 5/6 and 7/8 combination classes. Some students benefit from the review, and others benefit from the exposure to new material.

NOTE

Most students will find oral mental math difficult for a few weeks until they become familiar with the vocabulary and math methods necessary for success. When you correct the quizzes each day, it is essential that you show students on the board the easy way to solve the problems. Impress upon them the importance of learning vocabulary and math facts by heart.

You have choices about how to use this book. You may go through it sequentially or you may use questions from different pages to introduce or enhance a concept your class is studying. For example, if you were studying geometry, you could easily find geometry questions, using the chart on page 10.

What Students Need to Know to Do Mental Math on page 7 explains what the kids will need to learn while doing these mental math activities. Most of them can be explained during the time you correct the answers on the board each day, but some may need to be presented as a lesson from a math book or the teacher.

A "get-started list" of *Mental Math Facts* on page 9 has been provided. It contains measurements, geometric terms, and Roman numerals. Pass it out to students to keep, and encourage them to memorize the information on it. Be sure to explain anything students seem unsure of.

Finally, there are 15 different answer sheets with information to reinforce or introduce new or difficult math concepts visually throughout the year. Choose the answer sheets that will best help your students learn or reinforce math during each week. Photocopy two of the answer sheets back-to-back to save paper. Enjoy!

What Students Need to Know to Do Mental Math

✔ MATH VOCABULARY

- Sum, difference, product, quotient, factor
- Parallel lines, intersecting lines, right angle, circle, radius, diameter, circumference, triangle, equilateral triangle, rectangle, parallelogram, square, pentagon, hexagon, octagon, perimeter, area
- Decimal, common fraction, improper fraction, mixed number, percent
- Integer, algebraic equation

✔ MATH FACTS

- Addition, subtraction, and multiplication facts by heart

✔ UNDERSTANDING HOW THE NUMBER SYSTEM WORKS

- Each number column to the left is ten times larger than the one on the right. The reverse is also true—each number column to the right is one-tenth as large as the one on the left
- How to write numbers properly from trillions to hundredths
- Multiplying by 10, 100, or 1,000 (or higher) by just putting the proper amount of zeros before the one's column or moving the decimal point to the right the proper amount of columns

✔ FRACTIONS, DECIMALS & PERCENTS

- What amount a fraction or decimal represents
- Being able to express and understand the relationship between common fractions in all 3 of these forms: $1/2$, .5, and 50%
- That $2/3$ of something is just twice as much as $1/3$ of something
- That $3/4$ of something is the same as 75% (or $75/100$) of something
- That $1/2$, $5/10$, $6/12$, and $15/30$ all represent the same amount of something
- That our money system is the best way to understand decimals to hundredths
- That the metric system is designed so you can perform all conversions in your head by just moving the decimal point the proper amount of columns in the proper direction

✔ COMMON MEASUREMENTS

- Seconds, minutes, hours, days, weeks, months, seasons, years, decades, centuries, millenniums
- Inches, feet, yards, miles
- Cups, pints, quarts, gallons
- Ounces, pounds, tons
- Millimeters, centimeters, meters, kilometers
- Milliliters, liters
- Grams, kilograms, tonnes

✔ MENTAL SUBTRACTION

- With money problems like $15.00 - $6.15, subtract the whole dollars down to $1 above the amount with cents ($15 - $7 = $8); then subtract the remaining cents from the last dollar to get the rest of the answer ($1.00 - 15¢ = 85¢); and add the two ($8.85)
- With large numbers like 580 - 395, add 5 to the 395 to make 400, then subtract 580 - 400 to get 180, then add 5 to that answer to get 185
- If the problem were 580 - 375, simply subtract 500 - 300 and then 80 - 75 to get 200 + 5, or 205

✔ ADDING AND MULTIPLYING BEGINNING WITH THE LARGEST COLUMN

- To mentally compute 3 x 135, think 3 x 100 = 300; 3 x 30 =90; and 3 x 5 = 15; then 300 + 90 + 15 can easily be added mentally
- When adding two numbers like 234 and 556, add 200 + 500 first to get 700; add 30 + 50 to get 80; and add 4 + 6 to get 10; then combine 700 + 80 + 10 to get the sum mentally

✔ ROUNDING UP AND THEN SUBTRACTING HOW MUCH YOU ROUNDED UP

- 299 + 299 is just (300 - 1) + (300 - 1), which is (600 - 2), which is 598. Similarly, 6 x 295 is more simply solved by thinking (6 x 300) - (6 x 5), which is (1800 - 30), or 1770 (or 1,770).

✔ DIVIDING THE LARGER PART OF A NUMBER FIRST

- 36,540 ÷ 9 is quite easy to calculate mentally: 36,000 ÷ 9 is 4,000; and 540 ÷ 9 is 60; hence, the answer is 4,000 + 60, or 4,060

✔ MULTIPLYING WITH ZEROS

- This is the easiest of all shortcuts: 300 x 4,000 is simply solved by multiplying the two whole numbers (3 x 4), which equal 12, and then adding up the total number of zeros in the problem and tacking them behind the 12, being careful to place the right amount of commas in the right places—1,200,000.

✔ USING WHAT YOU KNOW TO SOLVE SOMETHING THAT LOOKS COMPLICATED

- Almost all kids know that 4 x 25 = 100, so why would 12 x 25 be a problem? It's just (4 x 25) + (4 x 25) + (4 x 25), or 100 + 100 + 100, or 300. So a problem like 19 x 25 is merely 4 (4 x 25)'s and 1 (3 x 25) or 400 + 75, or 475. The inches in 13 feet is merely the inches in 10 feet (120) + the inches in 3 feet (36), or 120 + 36, which is 156 inches!

Mental Math Facts

LENGTH COMPARISONS

- 12 inches = 1 foot
- 3 feet = 1 yard
- 5,280 feet = 1 mile
- 10 millimeters = 1 centimeter
- 100 centimeters = 1 meter
- 1,000 meters = 1 kilometer
- 1 inch = 2.5 centimeters
- 39 1/4 inches = 1 meter
- 1 mile = 1.6 kilometers

VOLUME

- 2 cups = 1 pint
- 2 pints = 1 quart
- 4 quarts = 1 gallon
- 1 cubic centimeter (1 cc) = 1 milliliter
- 1,000 milliliters = 1 liter
- 1.1 quarts = 1 liter

MASS (WEIGHT)

- 16 ounces = 1 pound
- 2,000 pounds = 1 ton
- 2.2 pounds = 1 kilogram
- 1.1 tons = 1 tonne
- 1 cc of water weighs 1 gram
- 1 liter of water weighs 1 kilogram
- 1,000 grams = 1 kilogram
- 1,000 kilograms = 1 tonne

ROMAN NUMERALS

1 = I	5 = V	9 = IX	14 = XIV	50 = L	500 = D
2 = II	6 = VI	10 = X	19 = XIX	80 = LXXX	1,000 = M
3 = III	7 = VII	11 = XI	20 = XX	90 = XC	5,000 = $\overline{V}$
4 = IV	8 = VIII	12 = XII	40 = XL	100 = C	10,000 = $\overline{X}$

Specific Math Subjects by Weeks

- ADDITION PATTERNS
1, 2, 4, 8, 10, 11, 12, 15, 16, 23, 24, 26, 29

- ALGEBRAIC EQUATIONS
47, 48, 49, 50

- AVERAGES
43, 44, 45

- DECIMALS
23, 27, 42

- DEGREES
45, 47

- DIVISION
6, 10, 11, 16, 17, 18, 24, 25, 26, 27, 31,
33, 37, 38, 41, 45

- FACTORS
8, 25, 26, 33, 50

- FRACTIONS
2, 11, 12, 14, 19, 20, 21, 22, 25, 27,
28, 29, 31, 34, 36, 39, 40, 41, 42, 43,
44, 44, 48, 50

- GEOMETRY
2, 6, 15, 29, 33, 34, 35, 37, 39, 40, 42,43

- GEOMETRIC FORMULAS
43, 44

- GREATER OR LESSER
6, 9, 14, 21, 22, 31, 32, 33, 35, 36, 42, 46,
47, 49

- HOW MANY?
1, 4, 7, 10, 11, 12, 15, 17, 18

- INTEGERS
46, 47, 49, 50

- MEASUREMENT
9, 10, 11, 12, 14, 15, 16, 17, 20, 23, 24, 25,
27, 30, 32, 33, 35, 36, 37, 39, 46, 47, 48

- MONEY
2, 3, 112, 13, 14, 17, 18, 19, 20, 21, 22, 25, 26,
27, 30, 34, 36, 37, 38, 41, 42

- MULTIPLICATION
2, 3, 5, 6, 8, 9, 11, 12, 13, 16, 17, 18, 19, 20,
23, 25, 26, 28, 29, 30

- NUMERATION
1, 3, 4, 5, 8, 9, 15, 17, 18, 32

- PATTERNS
1, 2, 11, 12, 17, 18, 19, 20, 21, 22, 23, 24, 27,
28, 29, 30, 31, 33, 34, 37, 38, 49, 50

- PERCENTS
27, 34, 35, 41

- PRIME NUMBERS
33, 34, 35, 36

- RANGE / MODE / MEDIAN / MEAN
45, 46, 47, 48

- RATIO
21, 22, 37, 38, 48, 49, 50

- ROMAN NUMERALS
13, 28, 29

- ROUNDING
7, 26, 27

- SQUARE ROOTS
10, 13, 15, 26, 45, 46, 47

- SQUARING & CUBING
18, 19, 26, 28, 29, 37, 38, 43, 44

- SUBTRACTION
4, 8, 11, 12, 20, 24, 30, 37, 38, 39

- TERMINOLOGY
7, 13, 23, 24, 27, 36, 37, 38, 39, 40

- TIME
9, 19, 21, 22, 23, 24, 25, 28

Week 1 Questions

MONDAY *Write the Number*

1. Write the number 91.
2. Write the number 901.
3. Write the number 910.
4. Write the number 9,001.
5. Write the number 9,010.
6. Write the number 53.
7. Write the number 503.
8. Write the number 530.
9. Write the number 5,003.
10. Write the number 50,303.

TUESDAY *Numeration*

1. $500 + 50 + 5 = ?$
2. $600 + 50 + 6 = ?$
3. $100 + 90 + 8 = ?$
4. $800 + 40 + 7 = ?$
5. $900 + 9 = ?$
6. $1,000 + 400 + 3 = ?$
7. $2,000 + 700 + 90 = ?$
8. $6,000 + 60 + 6 = ?$
9. $10,000 + 200 + 30 + 4 = ?$
10. $10,000 + 2,000 + 300 + 40 + 5 = ?$

THURSDAY *How Many?*

1. How many hours in a day?
2. How many days in a year?
3. How many socks in a pair?
4. How many socks in 3 pairs?
5. How many nickels in a quarter?
6. How many dimes in a dollar?
7. How many dimes in a half-dollar?
8. How many pennies in a dollar?
9. How many pennies in a half-dollar?
10. How many quarters in a dollar?

WEDNESDAY *How Many?*

1. How many sides on a triangle?
2. How many cents in a dollar?
3. How many dimes in a dollar?
4. How many quarters in a dollar?
5. How many sides on a square?
6. How many sides on a circle?
7. How many days in a week?
8. How many months in a year?
9. How many inches in a foot?
10. How many feet in a yard?

FRIDAY *More Than . . .*

1. What number is 2 more than 35 ?
2. What number is 3 more than 41 ?
3. What number is 4 more than 15 ?
4. What number is 5 more than 19 ?
5. What number is 6 more than 25 ?
6. What number is 7 more than 35 ?
7. What number is 8 more than 42 ?
8. What number is 9 more than 51 ?
9. What number is 10 more than 90 ?
10. What number is 100 more than 9 ?

Week 2 Questions

MONDAY *2 Times*

1. 2 x 0 = ?
2. 2 x 3 = ?
3. 2 x 6 = ?
4. 2 x 10 = ?
5. 2 x 20 = ?
6. 2 x 40 = ?
7. 2 x 50 = ?
8. 2 x 60 = ?
9. 2 x 100 = ?
10. 2 x 200 = ?

TUESDAY *Addition Patterns*

1. 3 + 3 = ?
2. 30 + 30 = ?
3. 300 + 300 = ?
4. 50 + 50 = ?
5. 500 + 500 = ?
6. 5,000 + 5,000 = ?
7. 9 + 9 = ?
8. 90 + 90 = ?
9. 900 + 900 = ?
10. 9,000 + 9,000 = ?

WEDNESDAY *How Many?*

1. Add 50 cents and 20 cents.
2. Add 30 cents and 50 cents.
3. Subtract 50 cents from 80 cents.
4. Subtract 90 cents from 1 dollar.
5. Multiply 20 cents by 3.
6. Multiply 10 cents by 4.
7. Multiply 20 cents by 5.
8. Divide 50 cents by 5.
9. Divide 40 cents by 2.
10. Divide 1 dollar by 4.

THURSDAY *Fraction Problems*

1. What is one-half of 10 ?
2. What is one-half of 20 ?
3. What is one-half of 100 ?
4. What is one-half of 1,000 ?
5. What is one-third of 30 ?
6. What is one-third of 300 ?
7. What is one-third of 3,000 ?
8. What is one-fourth of 400 ?
9. What is one-fourth of 4,000 ?
10. What is one-fourth of 40,000 ?

FRIDAY *Geometric Addition*

1. One triangle has how many sides?
2. One square has how many sides?
3. One circle has how many sides?
4. 1 square + 1 triangle have how many sides in all?
5. 1 triangle + 1 circle have how many sides in all?
6. 3 triangles have how many sides in all?
7. 10 triangles have how many sides in all?
8. 5 squares have how many sides in all?
9. 10 circles have how many sides in all?
10. 2 triangles + 2 squares + 2 circles have how many sides in all?

Week 3 Questions

MONDAY *Number & Numeration*
1. Write the number 803.
2. Write the number 8,003.
3. Write the number 80,003.
4. Write the number 80,303.
5. Write the number 800,300.
6. 600 + 80 + 4 = ?
7. 900 + 70 + 3 = ?
8. 7,000 + 600 + 5 = ?
9. 40,000 + 3,000 + 200 + 10 = ?
10. 500,000 + 500 + 5 = ?

TUESDAY *Doubles and Triples*
1. Double the number 20.
2. Triple the number 20.
3. Double the number 200.
4. Triple the number 300.
5. Double the number 2,000.
6. Double the number 25.
7. Double the number 50.
8. Double the number 75.
9. Triple the number 3,000.
10. Triple the number 3,333.

WEDNESDAY *Money*
1. What 3 coins make 30¢ ?
2. What 2 coins make 50¢ ?
3. What 3 coins make 12¢ ?
4. What 4 coins make 12¢ ?
5. What 3 coins make 25¢ ?
6. What 5 coins make 25¢ ?
7. What 7 coins make 25¢ ?
8. What 8 coins make 25¢ ?
9. What 9 coins make 25¢ ?
10. What 13 coins make 25¢ ?

THURSDAY *What's the Price?*
1. 2 packs of gum at 40¢ apiece?
2. 3 chocolate bars at 50¢ apiece?
3. 2 hamburgers at $1.50 apiece?
4. 2 sodas at 75¢ apiece?
5. 4 bags of candy at 50¢ apiece?
6. 5 popsicles at 40¢ apiece?
7. 10 snowcones at $1.00 each?
8. 6 bags of french fries at 60¢ each?
9. 3 milk shakes at $1.50 each?
10. 2 pepperoni pizzas at $9.00 each?

FRIDAY *What Is ...*
1. What is the 3rd day of the week?
2. What is the 3rd month of the year?
3. What is the 3rd planet from the sun?
4. What is the 6th day of the week?
5. What is the 5th month of the year?
6. What is the 4th planet from the sun?
7. What month always has the fewest days?
8. What is the number of seconds in a minute?
9. What is the number of minutes in an hour?
10. What is the number of hours in a day?

Week 4 Questions

MONDAY *How Many?*

1. How many 5's in 20 ?
2. How many 6's in 12 ?
3. How many 5's in 30 ?
4. How many 6's in 24 ?
5. How many 3's in 9 ?
6. How many 9's in 18 ?
7. How many 7's in 14 ?
8. How many 7's in 21 ?
9. How many 10's in 50 ?
10. How many 10's in 100 ?

TUESDAY *Addition*

1. $3 + 3 + 3 + 1 = ?$
2. $1 + 4 + 5 + 6 = ?$
3. $4 + 5 + 6 + 10 = ?$
4. $1 + 9 + 11 = ?$
5. $5 + 5 + 7 + 3 = ?$
6. $5 + 4 + 1 + 8 = ?$
7. $14 + 6 + 11 + 9 = ?$
8. $20 + 20 + 15 = ?$
9. $20 + 15 + 5 = ?$
10. $20 + 30 + 11 = ?$

WEDNESDAY *Next Number*

1. 2, 4, 6, ___
2. 5, 10, 15, ___
3. 3, 6, 9, ___
4. 10, 8, 6, ___
5. 20, 18, 16, ___
6. 50, 40, 30, ___
7. 900, 800, 700, ___
8. 200, 400, 600, ___
9. 250, 500, 750, ___
10. 500, 1,000, 1,500, ___

THURSDAY *Inverse of Addition*

1. If $2 + 8 = 10$, then $10 - 8 = ?$
2. If $3 + 7 = 10$, then $10 - 7 = ?$
3. If $6 + 6 = 12$, then $12 - 6 = ?$
4. If $3 + 9 = 12$, then $12 - 9 = ?$
5. If $6 + 9 = 15$, then $15 - 9 = ?$
6. If $20 + 30 = 50$, then $50 - 30 = ?$
7. If $200 + 400 = 600$, then $600 - 400 = ?$
8. If $3,000 + 7,000 = 10,000$ then $10,000 - 7,000 = ?$
9. If $40,000 + 50,000 = 90,000$, then $90,000 - 50,000 = ?$
10. If $2,000,000 + 6,000,000 = 8,000,000$, then $8,000,000 - 6,000,000 = ?$

FRIDAY *How Many?*

1. How many planets in the solar system?
2. How many states in the United States?
3. How many inches in a foot?
4. How many feet in a yard?
5. How many inches in a yard?
6. How many centimeters in a meter?
7. How many meters in a kilometer?
8. How many pounds in a ton?
9. How many days in a year?
10. How many days in April?

Week 5 Questions

MONDAY *Doubling*
1. $15 + 15 = ?$
2. $2 \times 15 = ?$
3. $20 + 20 = ?$
4. $2 \times 20 = ?$
5. $30 + 30 = ?$
6. $2 \times 30 = ?$
7. $400 + 400 = ?$
8. $2 \times 400 = ?$
9. $5{,}000 + 5{,}000 = ?$
10. $2 \times 5{,}000 = ?$

TUESDAY *Multiplication Extensions*
1. $3 \times 3 = ?$
2. $3 \times 300 = ?$
3. $4 \times 4 = ?$
4. $4 \times 400 = ?$
5. $5 \times 5 = ?$
6. $5 \times 500 = ?$
7. $2 \times 2{,}000 = ?$
8. $3 \times 3{,}000 = ?$
9. $4 \times 4{,}000 = ?$
10. $5 \times 5{,}000 = ?$

WEDNESDAY *Mixed Operations and Terminology*
1. Find the sum of 10, 5, and 6.
2. Find the difference between 11 and 4.
3. Find the sum of 15 and 20.
4. Find the difference between 15 and 20.
5. Find the number that is halfway between 30 and 50.
6. Find the number halfway between 100 and 200.
7. The product of $4 \times 10 = ?$
8. The dividend of 12 divided by 3 is?
9. The dividend of 100 divided by 4 is?
10. The product of 100×6 is?

THURSDAY *Write the Number*
1. 1 hundred, 8 tens, 3 ones.
2. 3 hundreds, 5 tens, 9 ones.
3. 2 hundreds, 2 ones.
4. 1 thousand, 4 hundreds, 8 tens, 6 ones.
5. 9 thousands, 5 tens.
6. 5 hundreds, 0 tens, 9 ones.
7. 1 hundred thousand, 5 ten thousands, 8 thousands, 6 hundreds, 3 tens.
8. 3 ten thousands, 6 thousands, 2 hundreds, 8 ones.
9. 2 millions, 5 hundred thousands, 9 ten thousands, 3 one thousands, 4 hundreds, 6 tens.
10. 9 millions, 9 thousands, 9 ones.

FRIDAY *Sports Math*
1. How many points for a free throw in basketball?
2. How many points for a regular basket in basketball?
3. How many points for a basket from half court?
4. How many outs does a team have in an inning?
5. How many strikes and you're out in baseball?
6. How many balls until you get a walk in baseball?
7. If a baseball game is 9 innings, how many outs does *each* team have for the entire game?
8. In football, you can get a new first down every how many yards?
9. In football, how many points do you get for a touchdown plus the extra point?
10. In soccer, how many points do you get for each goal?

Week 6 Questions

MONDAY *Multiplication Facts*

1. 5 x 3 = ?
2. 4 x 6 = ?
3. 6 x 6 = ?
4. 7 x 3 = ?
5. 3 x 8 = ?
6. 5 x 4 = ?
7. 4 x 7 = ?
8. 5 x 5 = ?
9. 4 x 4 = ?
10. 9 x 3 = ?

TUESDAY *How Many?*

1. How many 10's make 100 ?
2. How many 100's make 1,000 ?
3. How many 4's make 40 ?
4. How many 10's make 200 ?
5. How many 20's make 100 ?
6. How many 5's make 50 ?
7. How many 5's make 100 ?
8. How many 2's make 20 ?
9. How many 2's make 30 ?
10. How many 2's make 50 ?

WEDNESDAY *More or Less*

1. Which is more ... 4 x 7 *or* 3 x 10 ?
2. Which is more ... 5 x 4 *or* 3 x 6 ?
3. Which is more ... 3 x 8 *or* 5 x 5 ?
4. Which is more ... 4 x 4 *or* 3 x 5 ?
5. Which is more ... 2 x 11 *or* 5 x 4 ?
6. Which is less ... 5 x 5 *or* 3 x 10 ?
7. Which is less ... 8 x 4 *or* 2 x 12 ?
8. Which is less ... 6 x 6 *or* 7 x 5 ?
9. Which is less ... 5 x 10 *or* 7 x 7 ?
10. Which is less ... 9 x 2 *or* 4 x 5 ?

THURSDAY *Geometric Shapes*

1. A triangle has how many sides?
2. A square has how many sides?
3. A circle has how many sides?
4. A rectangle has how many sides?
5. A pentagon has how many sides?
6. A hexagon has how many sides?
7. An octagon has how many sides?
8. An oval has how many sides?
9. A trapezoid has how many sides?
10. A heptagon has how many sides?

FRIDAY *Halves of Things*

1. How many minutes in a half hour?
2. How many inches in half a foot?
3. How many centimeters in half a meter?
4. How many months in half a year?
5. How many pennies in half a dollar?
6. How many nickels in half a dollar?
7. How many dimes in half a dollar?
8. How many eggs in half a dozen?
9. How many years in half a century?
10. How many days in half a week?

Week 7 Questions

MONDAY *10's and 20's*
1. 20 + 10 = ?
2. 20 + 20 = ?
3. 20 - 10 = ?
4. 20 - 20 = ?
5. 10 x 10 = ?
6. 10 x 20 = ?
7. 20 x 20 = ?
8. 20 ÷ 10 = ?
9. 20 ÷ 20 = ?
10. 20 - 10 + 20 - 10 = ?

TUESDAY *Rounding to Nearest 10*
1. Round 38 to the nearest 10.
2. Round 52 to the nearest 10.
3. Round 9 to the nearest 10.
4. Round 87 to the nearest 10.
5. Round 55 to the nearest 10.
6. Round 64 to the nearest 10.
7. Round 19 to the nearest 10.
8. Round 3 to the nearest 10.
9. Round 76 to the nearest 10.
10. Round 95 to the nearest 10.

WEDNESDAY *How Many?*
How many...
1. ... eggs in a dozen?
2. ... months in a year?
3. ... days in 3 weeks?
4. ... days in 10 weeks?
5. ... days in a year?
6. ... days in a leap year?
7. ... wheels on a bicycle?
8. ... wheels on a tricycle?
9. ... wheels on a wagon?
10. ... legs on an octopus?

THURSDAY *Sums and Differences*
1. What is the sum of 9 and 7 ?
2. What is the difference between 9 and 7 ?
3. What is the sum of 25 and 15 ?
4. What is the difference between 25 and 15 ?
5. What is the sum of 34 and 14 ?
6. What is the difference between 34 and 14 ?
7. What is the sum of 350 and 150 ?
8. What is the difference between 350 and 150 ?
9. What is the sum of 5,500 and 3,500 ?
10. What is the difference between 5,500 and 3,500 ?

FRIDAY *Halves and Doubles*
1. One-half of 14 = ?
2. 2 x 14 = ?
3. One-half of 30 = ?
4. 2 x 30 = ?
5. One-half of 200 = ?
6. 2 x 200 = ?
7. One-half of 4,000 = ?
8. 2 x 4,000 = ?
9. One-half of 50,000 ?
10. 2 x 50,000 = ?

Week 8 Questions

MONDAY *Double, Triple & Quadruple*

1. Double 5.
2. Double 10.
3. Double 12.
4. Double 15.
5. Double 50.
6. Triple 20.
7. Triple 50.
8. Triple 200.
9. Quadruple 25.
10. Quadruple 100.

TUESDAY *Ordering Numbers From Smallest to Largest*

Order these numbers from smallest to largest.

1. 36, 60, 58
2. 99, 103, 101
3. 47, 36, 48
4. 70, 78, 91
5. 27, 18, 22
6. 178, 180, 184
7. 166, 161, 158
8. 535, 355, 553
9. 444, 404, 440
10. 980, 998, 890

WEDNESDAY *Equal or Not*

1. 30 = 15 + 15
2. 40 = 30 + 20
3. 50 = 35 + 20
4. 60 = 31 + 29
5. 55 = 30 + 25
6. 80 = 20 + 60
7. 90 = 40 + 50
8. 100 = 75 + 30
9. 25 = 15 + 20
10. 20 = 10 + 9 + 1

THURSDAY *Fun Days*

1. New Year's Day is January ___.
2. Groundhog's Day is February ___.
3. Valentine's Day is February ___.
4. St. Patrick's Day is March ___.
5. April Fool's Day is April ___.
6. Cinco de Mayo is on May ___.
7. Independence Day is July ___.
8. Halloween is October ___.
9. Thanksgiving Day is always on the ___Thursday of November.
10. New Year's Eve is December ___.

FRIDAY *Subtraction How Many Are Left?*

1. 2 dozen cookies - 4 = _____?
2. 3 dozen donuts - 6 = _____?
3. 1 foot - 2 inches = _____?
4. 3 feet - 6 inches = _____?
5. 1 dollar -1 quarter = _____?
6. 4 dollars - 4 quarters = _____?
7. 1 meter - 50 centimeters = _____?
8. 1 year - 3 months = _____?
9. 1 decade - 2 years = _____?
10. 1 century - 1 year = _____?

Triple 200?

MONDAY *Multiple Multiples*

1. 2 x 2 x 2 = ?
2. 3 x 3 x 3 = ?
3. 1 x 1 x 1 = ?
4. 4 x 3 x 2 x 1 = ?
5. 5 x 4 x 2 = ?
6. 4 x 5 x 3 = ?
7. 3 x 3 x 10 = ?
8. 5 x 5 x 10 = ?
9. 10 x 10 x 5 = ?
10. 10 x 10 x 10 = ?

TUESDAY *Next Number Please*

1. 3, 6, 9, 12, _____
2. 4, 8, 12, 16, _____
3. 35, 30, 25, 20, _____
4. 6, 12, 18, _____
5. 20, 40, 60, _____
6. 1, 3, 5, 7, _____
7. 100, 300, 500, 700, _____
8. 50, 100, 150, _____
9. 200, 400, 600, 800, _____
10. 1, 2, 4, 8, _____

WEDNESDAY *Which Is More?*

1. A kilogram *or* a pound?
2. A liter *or* a quart?
3. A centimeter *or* an inch?
4. 2 dozen *or* 5 x 5?
5. 5 nickels *or* 2 dimes?
6. 4 dozen *or* 5 x 10?
7. A kilometer *or* a mile?
8. 3 quarters *or* 8 dimes?
9. The days in January *or* the days in February?
10. A meter stick *or* a yardstick?

THURSDAY *What Makes What?*

1. 4 of these make a dollar.
2. 100 of these make a meter.
3. 1,000 of these make a kilometer.
4. 5,280 of these make a mile.
5. 100 of these make a dollar.
6. 365 of these make a year.
7. 12 of these make a year.
8. 24 of these make a day.
9. 60 seconds make one of these.
10. 30 days have September, April, June, and November. All the rest have 31 except _____.

FRIDAY *Squares*

Draw squares on the board showing how squares got their names: Multiply the side squares times the top squares to get the total number of squares.

1. 1 x 1 = ?
2. 2 x 2 = ?
3. 3 x 3 = ?
4. 4 x 4 = ?
5. 5 x 5 = ?
6. 6 x 6 = ?
7. 10 x 10 = ?
8. (2 x 2) + (4 x 4) = ?
9. (10 x 10) + (5 x 5) = ?
10. (3 x 3) + (4 x 4) = (? x ?)

Week 10 Questions

MONDAY *Halves & Thirds*

1. One half of the days in February?
2. One half of the years in a century?
3. One half of the states in the U.S.?
4. One third of the planets in our solar system?
5. One half of the months in a year?
6. One third of the months in a year?
7. One half of a dime?
8. One half of the pennies in $5.00 ?
9. One half of a quart of milk?
10. One half of the hours in a day?

TUESDAY *Square Roots*

1. 4 divided by 2 = ?
2. 9 divided by 3 = ?
3. 16 divided by 4 = ?
4. 25 divided by 5 = ?
5. 36 divided by 6 = ?
6. 49 divided by 7 = ?
7. 64 divided by 8 = ?
8. 81 divided by 9 = ?
9. 100 divided by 10 = ?
10. 144 divided by 12 = ?

WEDNESDAY *How Many?*

1. How many 10's are in 30 ?
2. How many 15's are in 30 ?
3. How many 2's are in 30 ?
4. How many 6's are in 30 ?
5. How many 5's are in 30 ?
6. How many 12's are in 36 ?
7. How many 5's are in 40 ?
8. How many 10's are in 60 ?
9. How many 6's are in 60 ?
10. How many 12's are in 60 ?

THURSDAY *True or False?*

1. February has 31 days in a leap year.
2. There are 36 inches in a yard.
3. A centimeter is larger than an inch.
4. You weigh objects in inches and feet.
5. There are 7 planets in our solar system.
6. October is the 8th month of the year.
7. July 4th is in the 2nd half of the 5th month.
8. Cinco de Mayo is on the 5th day of the 5th month.
9. On leap years, Thanksgiving moves to Friday.
10. In short years, December only has 30 days.

FRIDAY *How Many?—Just for Fun!*

1. 5 dogs have how many legs in all?
2. 3 octopi have how many legs in all?
3. 2 dogs + 2 octopi have how many legs in all?
4. 2 humans + 2 snakes + 3 octopi have how many legs in all?
5. 4 cows + 2 three-legged stools have how many legs in all?
6. 1 spider + 2 ants + 1 worm have how many legs in all?
7. 3 snakes + 2 worms + 4 sharks have how many legs in all?
8. 4 chickens + 3 dogs + 2 farmers have how many legs in all?
9. 100 spiders + 1 octopus have how many legs in all?
10. 1 centipede + 10 chickens + 4 humans have how many legs in all?

Week 11 Questions

MONDAY *Missing Addends*

1. $14 + ? = 18$
2. $15 + ? = 20$
3. $15 + ? = 21$
4. $17 + ? = 20$
5. $12 + ? = 24$
6. $10 + ? = 22$
7. $14 + ? = 24$
8. $? + 15 = 25$
9. $? + 13 = 25$
10. $? + 25 = 50$

TUESDAY *Missing Subtrahends*

1. $21 - ? = 11$
2. $22 - ? = 12$
3. $15 - ? = 10$
4. $19 - ? = 15$
5. $30 - ? = 20$
6. $50 - ? = 10$
7. $88 - ? = 78$
8. $44 - ? = 22$
9. $100 - ? = 50$
10. $200 - ? = 100$

WEDNESDAY *How Many?*

1. How many cents in a quarter?
2. How many dimes in a half-dollar?
3. How many planets in our solar system?
4. How many stripes on the U.S. flag?
5. How many stars on the U.S. flag?
6. How many colors on the U.S. flag?
7. How many days in a week?
8. How many weeks in a year?
9. How many days in a year?
10. How many seasons in a year?

THURSDAY *Fractions of . . .*

1. A day is what fraction of a week?
2. A nickel is what fraction of a dime?
3. A season is what fraction of a year?
4. A dime is what fraction of a dollar?
5. An egg is what fraction of a dozen?
6. A quarter is what fraction of a dollar?
7. A year is what fraction of a century?
8. A penny is what fraction of a nickel?
9. A penny is what fraction of a dime?
10. An inch is what fraction of a foot?

FRIDAY *Multiplication by 5's*

1. $5 \times 5 = ?$
2. $5 \times 10 = ?$
3. $5 \times 20 = ?$
4. $5 \times 50 = ?$
5. $5 \times 100 = ?$
6. $5 \times 200 = ?$
7. $5 \times 1,000 = ?$
8. $5 \times 10,000 = ?$
9. $5 \times 100,000 = ?$
10. $5 \times 1,000,000 = ?$

Week 12 Questions

MONDAY *Missing Addends*

1. $9 + ? = 29$
2. $19 + ? = 49$
3. $25 + ? = 65$
4. $60 + ? = 77$
5. $10 + ? = 31$
6. $20 + ? = 90$
7. $100 + ? = 400$
8. $? + 100 = 900$
9. $? + 1,000 = 5,000$
10. $? + 1,000,000 = 3,000,000$

TUESDAY *Missing Subtrahends*

1. $50 - ? = 10$
2. $1 - ? = 0$
3. $33 - ? = 11$
4. $66 - ? = 50$
5. $60 - ? = 30$
6. $100 - ? = 25$
7. $500 - ? = 450$
8. $1,000 - ? = 200$
9. $10,000 - ? = 7,000$
10. $1,000,000 - ? = 300,000$

WEDNESDAY *How Many?*

1. How many dimes in a dollar?
2. How many nickels in a dollar?
3. How many inches in a foot?
4. How many feet in a yard?
5. How many feet in a mile?
6. How many centimeters in a meter?
7. How many meters in 1 kilometer?
8. How many seconds in a minute?
9. How many minutes in an hour?
10. How many hours in a day?

THURSDAY *Fractions of. . .*

1. A quart is what fraction of a gallon?
2. A pint is what fraction of a quart?
3. A quarter is what fraction of a half-dollar?
4. A dollar is what fraction of a $10 bill?
5. An penny is what fraction of a dime?
6. A nickel is what fraction of a quarter?
7. A year is what fraction of a century?
8. 6 eggs are what fraction of a dozen?
9. 2 quarters are what fraction of a dollar?
10. 10 pennies are what fraction of 2 dimes?

FRIDAY *Multiplication by 3's and 4's*

1. $3 \times 50 = ?$
2. $4 \times 50 = ?$
3. $3 \times 500 = ?$
4. $4 \times 500 = ?$
5. $3 \times 5,000 = ?$
6. $4 \times 5,000 = ?$
7. $3 \times 50,000 = ?$
8. $4 \times 50,000 = ?$
9. $3 \times 500,000 = ?$
10. $4 \times 500,000 = ?$

Week 13 Questions

MONDAY *How Many?*

1. A square has how many sides?
2. A triangle has how many sides?
3. A circle has how many sides?
4. A rectangle has how many sides?
5. An octagon has how many sides?
6. How many days in a week?
7. How many days in January?
8. How many days in November?
9. How many days in a year?
10. How many days in a leap year?

TUESDAY *Multiplication Squares*

1. $3 \times 3 = ?$
2. $4 \times 4 = ?$
3. $5 \times 5 = ?$
4. $6 \times 6 = ?$
5. $7 \times 7 = ?$
6. $8 \times 8 = ?$
7. $9 \times 9 = ?$
8. $10 \times 10 = ?$
9. $20 \times 20 = ?$
10. $30 \times 30 = ?$

WEDNESDAY *Operations and Terminology*

1. The sum of 6 and 3 = ?
2. The difference between 6 and 3 = ?
3. The product of 6 and 3 = ?
4. The quotient of 6 divided by 3 = ?
5. The sum of 8 and 4 = ?
6. The difference between 8 and 4 = ?
7. The product of 8 and 4 = ?
8. The quotient of 8 divided by 4 = ?
9. The sum of 500 and 400 = ?
10. The product of 10 and 5 = ?

THURSDAY *Roman Numerals*

1. Write the Roman numeral 2.
2. Write the Roman numeral 3.
3. Write the Roman numeral 4.
4. Write the Roman numeral 5.
5. Write the Roman numeral 6.
6. Write the Roman numeral 8.
7. Write the Roman numeral 9.
8. Write the Roman numeral 10.
9. Write the Roman numeral 12.
10. Write the Roman numeral 15.

FRIDAY *Shopping*

1. Sal bought 3 candy bars at 50¢ apiece. How much did he spend?
2. Sally bought 2 magazines at $3.00 each. How much did she spend?
3. Ralph bought a $10 kite and a 50¢ ball of string. How much did he spend?
4. Ralpha bought 3 hair combs at $2.50 each. How much did she spend?
5. George bought 3 packs of baseball cards at $1.50 each. He paid with a $5.00 bill. How much change did he get?
6. Georgia bought 2 CDs at $8.00 each. She paid with a $20 bill. How much change did she get?
7. Marty got $50 dollars for his birthday. He bought a $39 baseball mitt. How much remained after buying the mitt?
8. Martha got $50 dollars for her birthday. She bought a new $42 soccer ball. How much remained after buying the ball?
9. Elmo bought a new $5 baseball and a $23 bat. He gave the clerk $30. How much change did he get?
10. Eleanor bought a used electric guitar for $85. She paid with a $100 bill. How much change did she get?

Week 14 Questions

MONDAY *Fractions*
Write True or False.
1. $1/2 + 1/2 = 1$
2. $1/4 + 1/4 = 1/2$
3. $1/3 + 2/3 = 3$
4. $1/2 - 1/4 = 1/4$
5. $1/2 + 1/4 + 1/8 = 1$
6. $3/10 + 7/10 = 1$
7. $5/10 + 4/10 + 2/10 = 1$
8. $1/2 + 1/2 + 1/4 = 2$
9. $1/3 + 2/3 + 3/3 = 2$
10. $1/2 + 1/4 + 1/8 + 1/16 = 1$

TUESDAY *Money Fractions*
Write Yes or No.
1. Is a quarter $1/2$ of a dollar?
2. Is a dime $1/10$ of a dollar?
3. Is a 50¢ coin $1/2$ of a dollar?
4. Is a nickel $1/2$ of a dime?
5. Is a nickel $1/5$ of a quarter?
6. Is a penny $1/100$ of a dollar?
7. Is a nickel $1/10$ of a dollar?
8. Is a dime $1/2$ of a quarter?
9. Is a quarter $1/3$ of 75¢?
10. Is a penny $1/10$ of 2 nickels?

WEDNESDAY *Which Is Larger?*
1. A centimeter or an inch?
2. A meter or a foot?
3. A meter or a yardstick?
4. A kilometer or a mile?
5. A gram or an ounce?
6. A kilogram or a pound?
7. A liter or a quart?
8. A liter or a gallon?
9. A metric tonne or a customary ton?
10. A hundred-yard race or a hundred-meter race?

THURSDAY *Add & Subtract—Money*
1. A dollar *minus* a half-dollar = ?
2. A quarter *minus* 2 dimes = ?
3. A half-dollar *minus* 2 quarters = ?
4. A half-dollar *minus* 2 dimes = ?
5. 3 quarters *minus* a nickel = ?
6. A dollar *minus* a nickel = ?
7. A quarter *plus* a dime *plus* a nickel = ?
8. 2 quarters *plus* 2 dimes = ?
9. 3 quarters *plus* 2 dimes *plus* a nickel = ?
10. One dollar *minus* a half-dollar *minus* a quarter *minus* a dime = ?

FRIDAY *Getting the Right Change*
1. Bob bought a football for $42. He gave he clerk $50 dollars. How much change should he get?
2. Bobbie bought a basketball for $34.50. She gave the clerk $35.00. How much change should she get?
3. Petra bought a new bike for $187. She gave the clerk $200. How much change should she get?
4. Pete bought some new soccer shoes for $83.50. He gave the clerk $85. How much change should he get?
5. Al bought a new watch for $44.50. He gave the clerk a $50 bill. How much change should he get?
6. Aline bought a new cheerleader outfit for $138. She gave the clerk $150. How much change should she get?
7. Charles bought 3 CDs. They each cost $12. He gave the clerk $40. How much change should he get?
8. Charlene bought 2 tickets for a rock concert. Each ticket cost $45. What change should she get if she paid with a $100 bill?
9. Jill's mom treated her 3 children to a movie. Each ticket cost $5. Mom gave them $20. How much money remains for treats?
10. Jeff bought a new CD player for $235. He also bought a $15 CD. He paid with $250. What was his change?

MONDAY *Writing Big Numbers*

1. 3,002
2. 5,602
3. 45,089
4. 97,130
5. 205,671
6. 891,043
7. 1,650,730
8. 3,078,654
9. 62,400,002
10. 123,456,789

TUESDAY *Multiple Addition*

1. 20 + 20 + 20 = ?
2. 30 + 30 + 30 = ?
3. 40 + 40 + 40 = ?
4. 50 + 50 + 50 = ?
5. 120 + 120 + 120 = ?
6. 150 + 150 + 150 = ?
7. 20 + 30 + 40 + 50 = ?
8. 30 + 70 + 40 + 60 = ?
9. 40 + 50 + 60 + 100 = ?
10. 10 + 20 + 30 + 40 = ?

WEDNESDAY *Square Roots*

1. What number divided by 1 = 1 ?
2. What number divided by 2 = 2 ?
3. What number divided by 3 = 3 ?
4. What number divided by 4 = 4 ?
5. What number divided by 5 = 5 ?
6. What number divided by 6 = 6 ?
7. What number divided by 7 = 7 ?
8. What number divided by 8 = 8 ?
9. What number divided by 9 = 9 ?
10. What number divided by 10 = 10 ?

THURSDAY *Geometry Figures*

1. Draw a circle.
2. Draw an oval.
3. Draw a square.
4. Draw a pentagon.
5. Draw a hexagon.
6. Draw a heptagon.
7. Draw an octagon.
8. Draw 2 parallel lines.
9. Draw 2 intersecting lines.
10. Draw a right angle.

FRIDAY *Halves of Things*

1. How many seconds in half a minute?
2. How many minutes in half an hour?
3. How many hours in half a day?
4. How many days in half of February?
5. How many months in half a year?
6. How many years in half a decade?
7. How many decades in half a century?
8. How many centuries in half a millennium?
9. How many dollars in half a million?
10. How many dollars in half a billion?

Week 16 Questions

MONDAY *Times Tables—Tough Ones*

1. 6 x 7 = ?
2. 9 x 4 = ?
3. 6 x 5 = ?
4. 7 x 8 = ?
5. 8 x 7 = ?
6. 9 x 7 = ?
7. 8 x 6 = ?
8. 6 x 9 = ?
9. 8 x 4 = ?
10. 9 x 8 = ?

TUESDAY *Division Facts*

1. 30 ÷ 6 = ?
2. 42 ÷ 6 = ?
3. 48 ÷ 6 = ?
4. 54 ÷ 6 = ?
5. 63 ÷ 7 = ?
6. 72 ÷ 8 = ?
7. 35 ÷ 7 = ?
8. 56 ÷ 8 = ?
9. 45 ÷ 9 = ?
10. 49 ÷ 7 = ?

WEDNESDAY *Adding 3 Numbers*

1. 20 + 30 + 5 = ?
2. 50 + 25 + 10 = ?
3. 60 + 30 + 10 = ?
4. 70 + 70 + 10 = ?
5. 100 + 50 + 25 = ?
6. 200 + 60 + 40 = ?
7. 300 + 200 + 80 = ?
8. 500 + 300 + 200 = ?
9. 6,000 + 5,000 + 400 = ?
10. 30,000 + 20,000 + 5,000 = ?

THURSDAY *How Many Make. . .*

1. 36 months make how many years?
2. 48 hours make how many days?
3. 360 seconds make how many minutes?
4. 28 days make how many weeks?
5. 60 inches make how many feet?
6. 15 feet make how many yards?
7. 600 centimeters make how many meters?
8. 3,000 meters make how many kilometers?
9. 1,000 grams make how many kilograms?
10. 12 quarts of milk make how many gallons?

FRIDAY *Bigger Units to Smaller Units*

1. 2 meters = how many centimeters?
2. 4 feet = how many inches?
3. 3 yards = how many feet?
4. 10 hours = how many minutes?
5. 3 gallons = how many quarts?
6. 2 years = how many months?
7. 4 meters = how many centimeters?
8. 3 kilograms = how many grams?
9. 5 tons = how many pounds?
10. 3 days = how many hours?

26

Week 17 Questions

MONDAY *Large Multiplication*

1. 50 x 6 = ?
2. 500 x 6 = ?
3. 5,000 x 6 = ?
4. 80 x 3 = ?
5. 800 x 3 = ?
6. 8,000 x 3 = ?
7. 40 x 9 = ?
8. 400 x 9 = ?
9. 4,000 x 9 = ?
10. 40 x 90 = ?

TUESDAY *Large Division*

1. 30 ÷ 6 = ?
2. 300 ÷ 6 = ?
3. 3,000 ÷ 6 = ?
4. 25 ÷ 5 = ?
5. 250 ÷ 5 = ?
6. 25,000 ÷ 5 = ?
7. 25,000,000 ÷ = ?
8. 100 ÷ 10 = ?
9. 1,000 ÷ 10 = ?
10. 100,000 ÷ 10 = ?

WEDNESDAY *Counting Backwards*

What's the next number?

1. 50, 45, 40, ____?
2. 50, 48, 46, ____?
3. 50, 40, 30, ____?
4. 100, 95, 90, ____?
5. 100, 80, 60, ____?
6. 100, 75, 50, ____?
7. 2,000; 1,800; 1,600; ____?
8. 3,000; 2,500; 2,000; ____?
9. 8,000; 7,800; 7,600; ____?
10. 1,000,000; 900,000; 800,000; ____?

THURSDAY *How Many?*

1. How many planets in our solar system?
2. How many stars in the Big Dipper?
3. How many inches in 3 feet?
4. How many feet in 5 yards?
5. How many months end with the letters "ber"?
6. How many months start with the letter "A"?
7. How many months have 31 days?
8. How many days in 5 weeks?
9. How many years in 2 decades?
10. How many hours in 2 days?

FRIDAY *Mixed Money Problems*

1. $5.00 - $3.50 = ?
2. $10.00 - $6.50 = ?
3. $12.50 + $3.50 = ?
4. $25.50 + $35.50 = ?
5. $4.25 x 4 = ?
6. $7.25 x 3 = ?
7. $8.00 ÷ 4 = ?
8. $10.00 ÷ 4 = ?
9. One-half of $24.24 = ?
10. One-half of $30.30 = ?

Week 18 Questions

MONDAY *Large Multiplication & Large Division*

1. 600 x 3 = ?
2. 6,000 x 3 = ?
3. 600 ÷ 3 = ?
4. 6,000 ÷ 3 = ?
5. 2,000 x 5 = ?
6. 20,000 x 5 = ?
7. 200 ÷ 5 = ?
8. 2,000 ÷ 5 = ?
9. 20,000 ÷ 5 = ?
10. 200,000 ÷ 5 = ?

TUESDAY *Squared Math Problems*

A number times itself is called a square.
($2^2 = 2$ x 2)

1. $2^2 + 2^2$ = ?
2. $2^2 + 3^2$ = ?
3. $3^2 + 4^2$ = ?
4. $5^2 + 2^2$ = ?
5. $5^2 - 4^2$ = ?
6. $6^2 + 2^2$ = ?
7. $7^2 + 1^2$ = ?
8. $7^2 - 3^2$ = ?
9. $10^2 - 1^2$ = ?
10. $10^2 + 5^2$ = ?

$$2^2 + 2^2 = ?$$

WEDNESDAY *Counting Backwards*

What's the next number?

1. 120, 115, 110, ____?
2. 320, 315, 310, ____?
3. 999, 888, 777, ____?
4. 908, 808, 708, ____?
5. 12,000; 11,500; 11,000; ____?
6. 30,000; 28,000; 26,000; ____?
7. 1,200; 1,100; 1,000; ____?
8. 450, 400, 350, ____?
9. 1,002; 1,001; 1,000; ____?
10. 1,000,000; 950,000; 900,000; ____?

THURSDAY *How Many?*

1. How many planets names begin with M?
2. How many months have just 30 days?
3. How many dimes in 2 dollars?
4. How many quarters in 3 dollars?
5. How many states in the United States?
6. How many continents are there?
7. How many letter "i"s in Mississippi?
8. How many letter "a"s in Alaska?
9. How many sides on a pentagon?
10. How many sides on an octagon?

FRIDAY *Mixed Money Problems*

1. $15.00 - $6.00 = ?
2. $15.50 + $6.50 = ?
3. $24.50 + $5.50 = ?
4. $24.50 - $5.50 = ?
5. $100 - $3 = ?
6. $100 x 3 = ?
7. $1,000 ÷ 5 = ?
8. $1,000 - $950 = ?
9. $1,000 - $650 = ?
10. $1,000.00 - $999.99 = ?

Week 19 Questions

MONDAY *Fractions*
Write True or False.

1. $1/2 = 2/4$
2. $1/2 = 3/6$
3. $1/2 = 4/10$
4. $1/2 = 50/100$
5. $1/2 = 5/8$
6. $1/2 = 1/4 + 1/4$
7. $1/2 = 2/10 + 3/10$
8. $1/2 = 3/8 + 1/8$
9. $1/2 = 2/10 + 4/10$
10. $1/2 = 500/1,000$

TUESDAY *2's Day*

1. $2 \times 20 = ?$
2. $2 \times 222 = ?$
3. $2 \times 202 = ?$
4. $2 \times 2,002 = ?$
5. $2 \times 22,222 = ?$
6. $2 + 20 + 200 + 2,000 = ?$
7. $2,000,000 + 2,000 + 2 = ?$
8. $2,222 - 200 = ?$
9. $22 + 22 + 22 = ?$
10. $222 + 222 + 222 = ?$

WEDNESDAY *Square Math*
Tell the students to multiply the squares and then add, subtract, or divide them.

1. $(10 \times 10) + (7 \times 7) = ?$
2. $(9 \times 9) - (1 \times 1) = ?$
3. $(8 \times 8) - (2 \times 2) = ?$
4. $(7 \times 7) + (1 \times 1) = ?$
5. $(6 \times 6) + (8 \times 8) = ?$
6. $(10 \times 10) \div (5 \times 5) = ?$
7. $(10 \times 10) \div (2 \times 2) = ?$
8. $(3 \times 3) + (4 \times 4) = ?$
9. $(9 \times 9) + (3 \times 3) = ?$
10. $(5 \times 5) + (5 \times 5) = ?$

THURSDAY *Buying Food*
Tell the students they can round off 99 cents to a dollar and then subtract a penny for each dollar after calculating the final cost.

1. 3 hot dogs at 80¢ each cost ___?
2. 5 fries at 50¢ each cost ___?
3. 2 milkshakes at 99¢ each cost ___?
4. 2 boxes of Cheerios at $3.99 each cost ___?
5. 4 quarts of milk at 99¢ each cost ___?
6. 5 packs of gum at 60¢ each cost ___?
7. 2 loaves of bread at $3.05 each cost ___?
8. 3 videos at $3.50 each cost ___?
9. 5 pounds of bananas at 99¢ a pound cost ___?
10. 7 potatoes at 40¢ each cost ___?

FRIDAY *Large Amounts of Time*
Remind students what decades, centuries, and millenniums are in years.

1. 1 century plus 5 decades is ? years.
2. 3 centuries and 7 decades is ? years.
3. 9 centuries and 9 decades is ? years.
4. A millennium is 1,000 years. How many years are in 1 $1/2$ millenniums?
5. A millennium plus 9 centuries is how many years?
6. A millennium plus 9 centuries plus 9 decades is how many years?
7. A millennium, 9 centuries, 9 decades, and 9 years is how many years?
8. The pyramids of Egypt were built 5 millenniums ago. How many years was that?
9. Ancient Greece was 2 and one-half millenniums ago. How many years was that?
10. Ancient humans existed 2,000 millenniums ago. How many years was that?

Week 20 Questions

MONDAY *Fractions: Subtracting*

1. $1 - 1/2 = ?$
2. $1 - 1/4 = ?$
3. $1 - 3/4 = ?$
4. $1 - 1/5 = ?$
5. $1 - 1/8 = ?$
6. $1 - 1/10 = ?$
7. $1 - 9/10 = ?$
8. $1 - 4/5 = ?$
9. $1 - 7/8 = ?$
10. $2 - 1/2 = ?$

TUESDAY *Multiplication Extensions*

1. $3 \times 20 = ?$
2. $3 \times 200 = ?$
3. $3 \times 2,000 = ?$
4. $4 \times 50 = ?$
5. $4 \times 500 = ?$
6. $4 \times 500,000 = ?$
7. $5 \times 60 = ?$
8. $5 \times 6,000?$
9. $5 \times 600,000 = ?$
10. $5 \times 6,000,000 = ?$

WEDNESDAY *Multiple Subtraction*

1. $20 - 5 - 5 - 5 = ?$
2. $30 - 3 - 3 - 3 = ?$
3. $40 - 10 - 10 - 10 = ?$
4. $50 - 15 - 15 = ?$
5. $60 - 15 - 15 - 15 = ?$
6. $70 - 20 - 20 - 20 = ?$
7. $80 - 25 - 25 - 25 = ?$
8. $90 - 30 - 30 - 30 = ?$
9. $100 - 20 - 20 - 20 = ?$
10. $500 - 50 - 50 - 50 = ?$

THURSDAY *Money Matters*

1. How many 35¢ donuts can you buy with $1.00?
2. How many 99¢ hotdogs can you buy with $5.00 ?
3. How many 40¢ bags of french fries can you buy with $2.00 ?
4. How many $2.99 books can you buy with $15.00 ?
5. How many $7.99 CDs can you buy with a $20.00 certificate?
6. How many $1.20 ice cream cones can you buy with $5.00 ?
7. How many $9.99 movie posters can you buy with $40.00 ?
8. How many $7.50 movie tickets can you buy with $30.00 ?
9. How many $3.50 video games can you rent with $10.00 ?
10. How could 3 friends evenly split $39 they found on the sidewalk?

FRIDAY *Fraction Problems*

1. $1/4$ of a year is how many months?
2. A month is what fraction of a year?
3. $1/2$ of a minute is how many seconds?
4. $1/4$ of an hour is how many minutes?
5. $1/3$ of an hour is how many minutes?
6. An inch is what fraction of a foot?
7. A foot is what fraction of a yard?
8. A centimeter is what fraction of a meter?
9. A quart is what fraction of a gallon?
10. What time would it be $2 \ 1/2$ hours after 7:00 a.m.?

MONDAY *Counting Money*

1. How many nickels in 45¢ ?
2. How many dimes in $1.80 ?
3. How many quarters in $5.00 ?
4. How many half-dollars in $50.00 ?
5. How many $2 bills in $60.00 ?
6. How many $5 bills in $100.00 ?
7. How many $10 bills in $250.00 ?
8. How many $20 bills in $300.00 ?
9. How many $50 bills in $900.00 ?
10. How many $100 bills in $2,000.00 ?

TUESDAY *Comparing Fractions*

Write Yes or No.

1. Is $1/3$ the same as $2/5$?
2. Is $1/3$ the same as $2/6$?
3. Is $1/4$ the same as $2/9$?
4. Is $1/5$ the same as $2/10$?
5. Is $1/6$ the same as $2/12$?
6. Is $1/10$ the same as $2/20$?
7. Is $1/2$ the same as $5/10$?
8. Is $1/3$ the same as $3/10$?
9. Is $1/4$ the same as $3/12$?
10. Is $1/5$ the same as $3/15$?

WEDNESDAY *Money Math*

1. 2 quarters - 3 dimes = ?
2. 3 quarters + 2 dimes = ?
3. 5 quarters - 2 dimes = ?
4. 6 quarters + 5 dimes = ?
5. 6 quarters - 5 dimes = ?
6. 10 quarters + 5 nickels = ?
7. 7 dimes - 2 quarters = ?
8. 3 quarters + 2 dimes + 1 nickel = ?
9. 3 quarters - 2 dimes - 1 nickel = ?
10. 4 quarters + 4 dimes + 4 nickels = ?

THURSDAY *Time Problems*

Tell the students to answer with *h* for hours and *m* for minutes (3*h* 15*m*). What are the hours and minutes between:

1. 9:30 a.m. and 10:10 a.m.?
2. 10:30 a.m. and 11:45 a.m.?
3. 8:15 a.m. and 10:00 a.m.?
4. 3:00 p.m. and 5:30 p.m.?
5. 5:30 p.m. and 9:00 p.m.?
6. 7:30 p.m. and midnight?
7. Midnight and 7:00 a.m.?
8. Noon and 3:15 p.m.?
9. Noon and midnight?
10. Midnight and noon?

FRIDAY *Halves and Fifths*

1. How much is $1/2$ of 12 ?
2. How much is $1/5$ of 20 ?
3. How much is $1/2$ of 30 ?
4. How much is $1/2$ of 200 ?
5. How much is $1/2$ of 1 ?
6. How much is $1/5$ of 25 ?
7. How much is $1/5$ of 250 ?
8. $1/2$ of a half-dollar is what coin?
9. $1/5$ of a half-dollar is what coin?
10. How much is $1/2$ of one million?

31

Week 22 Questions

MONDAY *More Money Problems*

1. How many quarters in $10.00 ?
2. How many dimes in $7.50 ?
3. How many nickels in 95 cents?
4. How many half-dollars in $75.00 ?
5. How many $5 bills in $200.00 ?
6. How many $2 bills in $80.00 ?
7. How many $10 bills in $650.00 ?
8. How many $20 bills in $1,000.00 ?
9. How many $50 bills in $1,000.00 ?
10. How many $100 bills in $10,000.00 ?

TUESDAY *Comparing More Fractions*

Write Yes or No.

1. Is $^1/_2$ the same as $^5/_{10}$?
2. Is $^1/_3$ the same as $^5/_{20}$?
3. Is $^1/_4$ the same as $^4/_{16}$?
4. Is $^1/_5$ the same as $^5/_{20}$?
5. Is $^1/_6$ the same as $^3/_{24}$?
6. Is $^1/_{10}$ the same as $^7/_{70}$?
7. Is $^1/_2$ the same as $^{50}/_{100}$?
8. Is $^1/_3$ the same as $^{30}/_{90}$?
9. Is $^1/_4$ the same as $^{12}/_{48}$?
10. Is $^1/_5$ the same as $^{12}/_{60}$?

WEDNESDAY *More Money Math*

1. 3 dollars + 3 quarters = ?
2. 8 dollars + 3 quarters = ?
3. 12 dollars - 6 dimes = ?
4. 15 dollars - 1 quarter - 5 dimes = ?
5. 20 dollars + 5 quarters + 5 nickels = ?
6. 30 dollars - 25 dollars - 4 dimes = ?
7. 52 dollars - 10 quarters = ?
8. 72 dollars + 2 quarters + 5 dimes = ?
9. 88 dollars + 8 quarters = ?
10. 88 dollars - 80 quarters = ?

THURSDAY *More Time Problems*

Tell the students to answer with *h* for hours and *m* for minutes (3*h* 15*m*). What are the hours and minutes between:

1. 7:00 a.m. and noon?
2. 7:00 a.m. and 1:00 p.m.?
3. 8:30 a.m. and noon?
4. 8:30 a.m. and 2:30 p.m.?
5. 12:15 p.m. and 2:45 p.m.?
6. 10:30 a.m. and 4:00 p.m.?
7. 11:30 a.m. and 5:00 p.m.?
8. Noon and 7:45 p.m.?
9. 11:00 p.m. and 7:00 a.m.?
10. 11:59 p.m. and midnight?

FRIDAY *More Halves and Fifths*

1. How much is $^1/_2$ of a century?
2. How much is $^1/_5$ of a decade?
3. How much is $^1/_2$ of a dollar?
4. How much is $^1/_5$ of a dollar?
5. How much is $^1/_2$ of $5 ?
6. How much is $^1/_5$ of $5 ?
7. How much is $^1/_2$ of $20 ?
8. How much is $^1/_5$ of $20 ?
9. How much is $^1/_2$ of $100 ?
10. How much is $^1/_5$ of $100 ?

MONDAY *Missing Addends*

1. $16 + ? = 20$
2. $110 + ? = 200$
3. $? + 180 = 200$
4. $? + 50 = 75$
5. $30 + ? = 80$
6. $30 + ? = 100$
7. $50 + ? = 250$
8. $300 + ? = 800$
9. $800 + ? = 1,100$
10. $30,000 + ? = 100,000$

TUESDAY *Multiplication Extensions*

Multiply the whole numbers and add the zeros.

1. $7 \times 30 = ?$
2. $7 \times 300 = ?$
3. $7 \times 3,000 = ?$
4. $7 \times 3,000,000 = ?$
5. $8 \times 60 = ?$
6. $8 \times 600 = ?$
7. $8 \times 6,000 = ?$
8. $8 \times 6,000,000 = ?$
9. $9 \times 900,000 = ?$
10. $9 \times 9,000,000 = ?$

WEDNESDAY *Fractions to Decimals*

The fraction $\frac{25}{100}$ = the decimal .25

1. $\frac{20}{100} = $ ___
2. $\frac{10}{100} = $ ___
3. $\frac{30}{100} = $ ___
4. $\frac{50}{100} = $ ___
5. $\frac{40}{100} = $ ___
6. $\frac{60}{100} = $ ___
7. $\frac{75}{100} = $ ___
8. $\frac{80}{100} = $ ___
9. $\frac{90}{100} = $ ___
10. $\frac{99}{100} = $ ___

THURSDAY *Operations Terminology*

1. What is the sum of 85 and 15?
2. What is the difference between 85 and 55?
3. What is the product of 30 and 5?
4. What is the quotient of 30 divided by 5?
5. What is 4 squared?
6. What is the square root of 25?
7. What is 50% of 100?
8. What is the difference between 32 and 22?
9. What is the perimeter of a rectangle whose sides are 5-inches long and 3-inches wide?
10. What is the area of a rectangle whose sides are 5-inches long and 3-inches wide?

FRIDAY *How Many—Time Problems*

1. How many hours in a day?
2. How many days in a regular year?
3. How many days in a leap year?
4. How many weeks in a year?
5. How many months in a year?
6. How many days in a week?
7. How many seasons in a year?
8. How many years in a decade?
9. How many years in a century?
10. How many years in a millennium?

Week 24 Questions

MONDAY *Missing Subtrahends*

1. 20 - ? = 16
2. 200 - ? = 110
3. 2,000 - ? = 1,100
4. 75 - ? = 30
5. 850 - ? = 825
6. 900 - ? = 870
7. 3,000 - ? = 2,400
8. 10,000 - ? = 5,500
9. 10,000 - ? = 9,500
10. 100,000 - ? = 85,000

TUESDAY *Division Extensions*

1. 21 ÷ 7 = ?
2. 210 ÷ 7 = ?
3. 2,100 ÷ 7 = ?
4. 35 ÷ 5 = ?
5. 350 ÷ 5 = ?
6. 3,500 ÷ 5 = ?
7. 81 ÷ 9 = ?
8. 810 ÷ 9 = ?
9. 81,000 ÷ 9 = ?
10. 81,000,000 ÷ 9 = ?

WEDNESDAY *Halves*

1. How many hours in half a day?
2. How many months in half a year?
3. How many months in half a leap year?
4. How many weeks in half a year?
5. How many days in half of February?
6. How many days in half of September?
7. How many seasons in half a year?
8. How many years in half a decade?
9. How many years in half a century?
10. How many years in half a millennium?

THURSDAY *Operations Terminology*

1. What is the product of 7 and 9 ?
2. What is the quotient of 50 divided by 10 ?
3. What is the difference between 37 and 20 ?
4. What is the sum of 57 and 40 ?
5. What is 6 squared?
6. What is the square root of 81 ?
7. What is 50% of 1,000 ?
8. What is the sum of 32 and 42 ?
9. What is the perimeter of a rectangle whose sides are 4-inches wide and 6-inches long?
10. What is the area of a rectangle whose sides are 7-inches long and 3-inches wide?

FRIDAY *What's More Than . . .*

1. What number is 40 more than 80 ?
2. What number is 50 more than 750 ?
3. What number is 200 more than 399 ?
4. What number is 25 more than 90 ?
5. What number is 55 more than 710 ?
6. What number is 33 more than 666 ?
7. What number is 99 more than 1,000 ?
8. What number is 500 more than 800 ?
9. What number is 6,000 more than 13,000 ?
10. What number is 50,000 more than 120,000 ?

MONDAY *Missing Factors*

1. $? \times 5 = 40$
2. $? \times 9 = 45$
3. $? \times 8 = 32$
4. $? \times 10 = 90$
5. $? \times 7 = 56$
6. $? \times 6 = 42$
7. $? \times 2 = 20$
8. $? \times 12 = 24$
9. $? \times 30 = 90$
10. $? \times 50 = 200$

TUESDAY *Fractions of Measurements*

1. $1/2$ of a ton = ? pounds
2. $1/2$ of a meter = ? centimeters
3. $1/2$ of a century = ? years
4. $1/4$ of a century = ? years
5. $3/4$ of a century = ? years
6. $3/4$ of a kilogram = ? grams
7. $1/2$ of a kilometer = ? meters
8. $1/4$ of a kilometer = ? meters
9. $1/10$ of a centimeter = ? millimeter
10. $9/10$ of a meter = ? centimeters

WEDNESDAY *Halfway*

1. What number is halfway between 0 and 20?
2. ? is halfway between 150 and 250.
3. ? is halfway between 100 and 500.
4. ? is halfway between 500 and 1,000.
5. ? is halfway between $1/4$ and $3/4$.
6. ? is halfway between $1/8$ and $5/8$.
7. ? is halfway between Monday and Friday.
8. ? is halfway between the year 1900 and 2000.
9. ? is halfway between 90° and 50°.
10. ? is halfway between April 1 and 30.

THURSDAY *Rounding 99 to 100*

Tell students to use the mental math skill of rounding 99¢ to $1.00 to add more easily in their heads. Once they have the total, then they subtract 1¢ for each $.

1. If 6 mini donuts cost 99¢, how much would 12 mini donuts cost?
2. If a box of cereal costs $2.99, how much would 2 boxes cost?
3. If you bought 4 ink pens at 99¢ apiece, how much did you spend?
4. If you bought 3 candy bars at 49¢ apiece, how much would they cost?
5. How much would 5 burgers at 99¢ cost?
6. 4 bags of french fries at 49¢ each would cost how much in all?
7. 10 packs of gum at 49¢ each cost?
8. If you bought 3 shirts at $9.99 each, how much would all three cost?
9. If you bought 2 pairs of shoes at $24.99 each, how much would both pairs cost?
10. You want 2 bicycles at $299.99 each. How much will both cost?

FRIDAY *Time for Time*

1. How many minutes are there between 9:15 a.m. and 11:45 a.m.?
2. How many hours are there between 8:00 a.m. and 7:00 p.m.?
3. How many hours in 2 days?
4. How many hours in 10 days?
5. How many weeks in any month?
6. If a baby is 24 months old, how many years old is it?
7. If you are 10 years old, how many months old are you?
8. If a student is 11 years old this year, what year was she born?
9. If someone is 100 years old this year, what year was he or she born?
10. What year will it be ten years from now?

MONDAY *More Missing Factors*

1. ? x 40 = 400
2. 50 x ? = 300
3. ? x 60 = 180
4. 4 x ? = 160
5. ? x 300 = 2,400
6. 8 x ? = 640
7. ? x 3,000 = 12,000
8. 9 x ? = 9,000
9. 2 x ? = 20,000
10. 10 x ? = 10,000,000

TUESDAY *Money Review*

1. 5 quarters + 2 dimes = ?
2. 1 half-dollar + 1 quarter + 1 dime = ?
3. One dollar - 3 quarters = ?
4. Two dollars - 3 quarters = ?
5. 16 dimes + 4 nickels = $?
6. $80.00 ÷ by 4 = $?
7. $80.00 x 4 = ?
8. $80.00 + $4.00 = ?
9. $80.00 - $4.00 = ?
10. How many half-dollars in $80 ?

WEDNESDAY *Halfway*

What is halfway between . . .

1. . . . 100,000 and 500.000 ?
2. . . . $300 and $400 ?
3. . . . $1/4$ and $3/4$?
4. . . . $2/5$ and $4/5$?
5. . . . Sunday and Saturday?
6. . . . April and June?
7. . . . 4 p.m. and 12 p.m. ?
8. . . . 9 feet and 3 feet?
9. . . . the year 1200 and the year 2000 ?
10. . . . 0 and 1,000,000 ?

THURSDAY *Squares & Square Roots*

5^2 is the same as 5 x 5. A square root is a number that is divided by a number that produces a quotient with the same number. 25 divided by 5 = 5.

1. $5^2 - 1^2 = ?$
2. $3^2 + 2^2 = ?$
3. $10^2 - 1^2 = ?$
4. $3^2 + 4^2 = ?$
5. $5^2 + 10^2 = ?$
6. What is the square root of 16 ?
7. What is the square root of 36 ?
8. What is the square root of 100 ?
9. What is the square root of 81 ?
10. What is the square root of 64 ?

FRIDAY *Round Off 99's to 100's or Thousands or More*

1. 99 + 99 = ? (i.e., 200)
2. 99 + 99 + 99 = ?
3. 999 + 999 = ?
4. 9,999 + 9,999 = ?
5. 99,999 + 99,999 = ?
6. 999,999 + 999,999 = ?
7. 9,999,999 + 9,999,999 = ?
8. How much would 2 motorcycles cost at $9,999 each?
9. How much would 2 condos cost at $89,999 each?
10. How much would 3 Rolls Royce automobiles cost at $199,999 each?

Week 27 Questions

MONDAY *Short Division*

Put on the board: $150 \div 3 = 50$
$153 \div 3 = 51$
$159 \div 3 = 53$

1. $18 \div 3 = ?$
2. $180 \div 3 = ?$
3. $183 \div 3 = ?$
4. $189 \div 3 = ?$
5. $21 \div 3 = ?$
6. $210 \div 3 = ?$
7. $213 \div 3 = ?$
8. $27 \div 3 = ?$
9. $270 \div 3 = ?$
10. $273 \div 3 = ?$

TUESDAY *Fractions to Decimals*

Put on the board: The fraction $^{25}/_{100}$ = the decimal .25

1. $^{20}/_{100}$ = ____
2. $^{10}/_{100}$ = ____
3. $^{30}/_{100}$ = ____
4. $^{50}/_{100}$ = ____
5. $^{40}/_{100}$ = ____
6. $^{60}/_{100}$ = ____
7. $^{75}/_{100}$ = ____
8. $^{80}/_{100}$ = ____
9. $^{90}/_{100}$ = ____
10. $^{99}/_{100}$ = ____

WEDNESDAY *Decimals to Percents*

Put on the board: .25 = 25%
(percent means per one hundred)

1. .20 = ____%
2. .10 = ____%
3. .30 = ____%
4. .50 = ____%
5. .40 = ____%
6. .60 = ____%
7. .75 = ____%
8. .80 = ____%
9. .90 = ____%
10. .99 = ____%

THURSDAY *25 and 5*

1. What's the difference between 25 and 5?
2. What's the sum of 20 and 5?
3. What's the product of 25 and 5?
4. What's the product of 250 and 5?
5. What's the quotient of 25 divided by 5?
6. What's the quotient of 250 divided by 5?
7. What's 250 minus 5?
8. What's 2,500 minus 5?
9. What's 250,000 divided by 5?
10. What's the product of 250,000 and 5?

FRIDAY *Spending Money—Rounding*

Remind students about rounding up a cent.

1. If a hamburger costs 99¢, about how much would it cost for 3 of them?
2. How much would an 89¢ soda and a 99¢ soda cost?
3. If 1 salad costs $2.99, how much would 3 salads cost?
4. Milkshakes are $1.49 each. How much would 3 cost?
5. A bag of fries are 49¢. How much would 6 bags of fries cost?
6. Pizzas are $9.99 each. How many would 3 pizzas cost?
7. Large special pizzas are $14.99 each. How much would 3 large special pizzas cost?
8. Hotdogs are 89¢ each. About how much will 4 hotdogs cost?
9. Ice cream cones are 79¢ a scoop. How much would a double scoop of ice cream cost?
10. Cherry sodas are $1.49 each. About how much would 4 cherry sodas cost?

Week 28 Questions

MONDAY *5 and 4*

1. 5 x 40 = ?
2. 5 x 400 = ?
3. 50 x 40 = ?
4. 50 x 400 = ?
5. 500 x 400 = ?
6. 500 x 4000 = ?
7. How many 50's in 400?
8. How many 500's in 4,000?
9. What is one-fifth of 40?
10. What is one-fifth of 40,000?

TUESDAY *Multiple Multiples*

1. 3 x 3 x 3 = ?
2. 4 x 4 x 10 = ?
3. 3 x 4 x 5 = ?
4. 3 x 4 x 10 = ?
5. 2 x 4 x 8 = ?
6. 3 x 5 x 10 = ?
7. 5 x 5 x 10 = ?
8. 2 x 5 x 100 = ?
9. 5 x 5 x 1,000 = ?
10. 10 x 100 x 1,000 = ?

WEDNESDAY *How Many?*

1. How many seconds in 1 minute?
2. How many seconds in 4 minutes?
3. How many minutes in 1 hour?
4. How many minutes in a half hour?
5. How many seconds in 10 minutes?
6. How many hours in a day?
7. How many hours in half a day?
8. How many hours in 10 days?
9. How many days in 3 weeks?
10. How many days in 11 weeks?

THURSDAY *Roman Numeral Math*

1. V x X = ?
2. X x X = ?
3. III x V = ?
4. X x L = ?
5. V x D = ?
6. D ÷ C = ?
7. M ÷ D = ?
8. M ÷ X = ?
9. XXX ÷ VI = ?
10. MMM ÷ V = ?

FRIDAY *Squares*

1. $5^2 + 1^2 = ?$
2. $10^2 - 7^2 = ?$
3. $10^2 - 8^2 = ?^2$ (What number squared?)
4. $6^2 - 2^2 = ?$
5. $8^2 - 2^2 = ?$
6. $9^2 + 3^2 = ?$
7. $10^2 + 5^2 = ?$
8. $5^2 - 1^2 =$ How many dozen?
9. $2^2 \times 5^2 = ?$
10. $3^2 + 4^2 = ?^2$ (What number squared?)

38

Week 29 Questions

MONDAY *Equal or Not*

1. 3 x 12 = 62
2. 2 x 12 = 52
3. 3 x 3 = 42
4. 81 - 72 = 32
5. 100 - 96 = 22
6. 3 x 50 = 2 x 70
7. 4 x 100 = 8 x 50
8. 33 x 3 = 100 - 1
9. 1,000 = 2 x 400
10. 1,000,000 ÷ 5 = 20,000

TUESDAY *Geometry Addition*

1. 5 triangles + 1 square = ? sides in all
2. 2 trapezoids + 1 circle = ? sides
3. 3 ovals + 6 rectangles = ? sides
4. 4 hexagons + 2 triangles = ? sides
5. 5 octagons + 2 pentagons = ? sides
6. 1 square + 3 ovals = ? sides
7. 10 triangles + 1 pentagon = ? sides
8. 4 pentagons + 4 heptagons = ? sides
9. 2 decagons + 2 nonagons = ? sides
10. 10 circles + 10 ovals = ? sides

WEDNESDAY *More Roman Math*
Answer in Roman numerals.

1. III + VIII = ?
2. XIII + VIII = ?
3. XXX ÷ V = ?
4. XX x V = ?
5. VI x C = ?
6. CCC ÷ V = ?
7. XIII + XV = ?
8. C - XV = ?
9. If C is 100, what is the square root of C?
10. Write one thousand, one hundred and eleven.

THURSDAY *More Roman Math*
Answer in Roman numerals.

1. X x V = ?
2. L ÷ V = ?
3. L - XX = ?
4. VII x C = ?
5. C - L = ?
6. C - XXX = ?
7. X x C = ?
8. M ÷ D = ?
9. X x X x X = ?
10. C x XXX = ?

FRIDAY *Multiples*

1. Double 750.
2. Triple 250.
3. Quadruple 1,000.
4. Quintuple 2,000.
5. Double 25,025.
6. Triple 33,333.
7. Quadruple 250,000.
8. Quintuple 2,000,000.
9. Double 5,000,005.
10. Triple 3,333,333.

Week 30 Questions

MONDAY *Double Multiplication*

Remind students they can do these problems by multiplying the 10's first, then the 1's, and finally adding the answers together.

1. 5 x 45 = ?
2. 6 x 51 = ?
3. 6 x 52 = ?
4. 7 x 51 = ?
5. 7 x 55 = ?
6. 8 x 35 = ?
7. 6 x 33 = ?
8. 9 x 21 = ?
9. 9 x 22 = ?
10. 6 x 66 = ?

TUESDAY *Customary Measurements*

1. 10,560 feet = ? miles
2. 48 inches = ? feet
3. 12 feet = ? yards
4. 240 minutes = ? hours
5. 12 quarts = ? gallons
6. 60 inches = ? yards
7. 4 pints = ? quarts
8. 21 feet = ? yards
9. 24 quarts = ? gallons
10. 600 minutes = ? hours

WEDNESDAY *How Much Change?*

1. $5.00 - $1.50 = ?
2. $10.00 - $4.99 = ?
3. $20.00 - $9.99 = ?
4. $50.00 - $35.00 = ?
5. $6.00 - $4.50 = ?
6. $3.00 - $1.98 = ?
7. $5.00 - $3.75 = ?
8. $10.00 - $7.50 = ?
9. $20.00 - $19.99 = ?
10. $100.00 - $69.00 = ?

THURSDAY *Inches, Feet, and Yards*

1. If 1 foot = 12 inches, how many inches in half a foot?
2. How many inches in 2 feet?
3. How many inches in a foot and a half?
4. How many inches in 3 feet?
5. How many inches in 6 feet?
6. If there are 36 inches in a yard, how many inches in $1/3$ of a yard?
7. How many inches in $2/3$ of a yard?
8. How many inches in half a yard?
9. How many inches in 2 yards?
10. How many feet in a yard?

FRIDAY *More Money Math*

1. If I spent $3.99, how much change would I get from $5.00 ?
2. If I spent $8.49, how much change would I get from a $10 bill?
3. If I had three $20 bills and two $5 dollar bills, would I have enough money to buy a $72 coat?
4. If I had two $20 bills and a $50 bill, could I buy a new pair of shoes that cost $84.99 ?
5. How many $5 bills make $40 ?
6. How many $10 bills make $770 ?
7. How many quarters make $100 ?
8. How many dimes make $3.70 ?
9. How many nickels make 65¢ ?
10. How many pennies make $20 ?

40

Week 31 Questions

MONDAY *Fractions of Large Numbers*
1. What is one-half of 700?
2. What is one-third of 600?
3. What is one-fourth of 120?
4. What is one-half of 22,000?
5. What is one-half of 1,000,000?
6. What is one-half of 900,000?
7. What is one-tenth of 3,000?
8. What is one-fifth of 1,000?
9. What is one-fourth of 500?
10. What is one-fourth of 12,000?

TUESDAY *Simple Fraction Problems*
1. $1/2$ minus $1/4$ = ?
2. $3/4$ minus $1/4$ = ?
3. $3/4$ plus $1/4$ = ?
4. $1/2$ plus $1/4$ = ?
5. $1/4$ plus $2\ 1/4$ = ?
6. $3/4$ minus $1/2$ = ?
7. $1/10$ plus $5/10$ = ?
8. $1/10$ plus $5/10$ = ?
9. $4/10$ plus $5/10$ = ?
10. $9/10$ minus $5/10$ = ?

WEDNESDAY *36 Divided*
1. 36 divided by 4 = ?
2. 360 divided by 4 = ?
3. 360 divided by 6 = ?
4. 3,600 divided by 6 = ?
5. 360 divided by 10 = ?
6. 360 divided by 36 = ?
7. 3,600 divided by 100 = ?
8. 36,000 divided by 1,000 = ?
9. 3,600,000 divided by 10 = ?
10. 36,000,000 divided by 6 = ?

THURSDAY *Who Am I?*
1. If I am squared, I am one less than half of a century.
2. When used as a factor to multiply, I never change the product.
3. We are 3 consecutive numbers who add up to 33. Who are we?
4. On a number line, I am half way between $1/2$ and one.
5. If the number of planets in our solar system were squared, there would be this number of planets.
6. When you add me or subtract me, the answer always remains the same.
7. When you multiply or divide with me, you always end up with me.
8. I am $1/12$ of a foot and $1/36$ of a yard.
9. I am 1,000 millimeters long or $1/1,000$ of a kilometer short.
10. I am a quarter of a gallon or a half of a half gallon.

FRIDAY *Which Is Greater?*
1. 92 *or* 9 x 10?
2. 3 x 20 *or* 5 x 11?
3. 6 x 50 *or* 360?
4. $1/2$ of 500 *or* $1/3$ of 900?
5. 8 x 50 *or* 4 x 90?
6. 26.9 *or* 28.1?
7. 3 quarts *or* one gallon?
8. 2 kilometers *or* 300 centimeters?
9. 5,000 pounds *or* 3 tons?
10. 2 $20 bills *or* 7 $5 bills?

Week 32 Questions

MONDAY *Knowing Numbers*

1. Write the number for 70,707.
2. Which column is the 6 in 95,642?
3. Write 67 in Roman numerals.
4. Write the fraction $^2/_5$.
5. What % is the same as 25 cents?
6. Write a fraction that equals 25%.
7. Count the next 3 numbers backwards from 100.
8. What fraction of a meter is 10 cm.?
9. Double 123.
10. Triple $^1/_4$.

TUESDAY *Metric Lengths*
Answer True or False.

1. 100 millimeters make a meter.
2. A millimeter is as wide as a hair.
3. 100 centimeters are in a meter.
4. A centimeter is about as wide as your pinky.
5. A millimeter is wider than a centimeter.
6. There are 100 meters in a kilometer.
7. 10 pro soccer fields = a kilometer.
8. $^6/_{10}$ of a mile = a kilometer.
9. A centimeter is longer than an inch.
10. A meter is longer than a yardstick.

WEDNESDAY *Comparing Measurement*
Answer True or False.

1. 10 millimeters = 1 centimeter
2. 1,000 centimeters makes a meter.
3. A meter is longer than a yardstick.
4. An inch is as wide as 2 $^1/_2$ centimeters.
5. 100 meters = 1 kilometer.
6. A kilometer weighs 2 metric tonnes.
7. A liter contains less than a quart.
8. A liter contains 1,000 milliliters.
9. A kilometer is 100 soccer fields long.
10. A kilogram is heavier than a pound.

THURSDAY *Which Is Larger?*

1. 8 x 7 *or* 5 x 11 ?
2. 3 x 12 *or* 2 x 13 ?
3. 62 *or* 7 x 5 ?
4. 92 *or* 90 ?
5. 32 *or* 8 ?
6. 5 dozen *or* 48 ?
7. A half dollar *or* 4 dimes and 11 pennies?
8. Roman numeral XVI *or* XIV ?
9. 150 minutes *or* 2 hours?
10. 9 centuries *or* a millennium?

FRIDAY *Who Am I?*

1. I am the square root of 64.
2. I am the number of days in December.
3. I am the number of degrees in a right angle.
4. I am the number of degrees in a circle.
5. I am the number of sides on a triangle.
6. I am the number of sides on an octagon.
7. I am the number of days in a regular year.
8. I am the number of weeks in a year.
9. I am the number of faces on a cube.
10. I am the number of faces on a cylinder.

Triple $^1/_4$ = ?

Week 33 Questions

MONDAY *Prime Numbers*

A prime number has only 2 factors, 1 times the number itself—(1 x 3 = 3). Non-prime numbers have several factors that can be multiplied to make the number—(1 x 4 and 2 x 2). See if you can identify prime numbers. Write Yes or No.

1. 5
2. 6
3. 7
4. 8
5. 9
6. 10
7. 11
8. 12
9. 13
10. 14

TUESDAY *How Many?*

1. How many 80's in 480 ?
2. How many 25's in 300 ?
3. How many 100's in 3,400 ?
4. How many quarters in $5 ?
5. How many dimes in $12.00 ?
6. How many half-dollars in $30 ?
7. How many $5 bills in $200 ?
8. How many pounds in 3 tons?
9. How many sides in a decagon?
10. How many faces on a cube?

WEDNESDAY *1 and $^1/_2$*

1. One and $^1/_2$ kilograms = ? grams.
2. One and $^1/_2$ meters = ? centimeters.
3. One and $^1/_2$ feet = ? inches.
4. One and $^1/_2$ yards = ? inches.
5. One and $^1/_2$ gallons = ? quarts.
6. One and $^1/_2$ kilometers = ? meters.
7. One and $^1/_2$ hours = ? minutes.
8. One and $^1/_2$ minutes = ? seconds.
9. One and $^1/_2$ centuries = ? years.
10. One and $^1/_2$ dollars = ? cents.

THURSDAY *Which Is Larger?*

1. 8 x 8 *or* 6 x 11
2. 3 x 120 *or* 2 x 130
3. 42 *or* 3 x 5
4. 82 *or* 50 + 15
5. 52 *or* $^1/_5$ of 100
6. 4 dozen *or* 72
7. 3 quarters *or* 7 dimes
8. The days in September *or* October
9. 175 minutes *or* 3 hours
10. 15 centuries *or* a millennium

FRIDAY *Who Am I?*

1. I am a rectangle—draw me.
2. I am a pentagon—draw me.
3. I am a right angle—draw me.
4. I am a semicircle—draw me.
5. I am a triangle—draw me.
6. I am an octagon—draw me.
7. I am an oval—draw me.
8. I am 2 parallel lines—draw me.
9. I am a hexagon—draw me.
10. Draw two intersecting lines.

Week 34 Questions

MONDAY *8 and 9*

1. $8 + 9 = ?$
2. $80 + 90 = ?$
3. $800 + 900 = ?$
4. $8 \times 9 = ?$
5. $80 \times 90 = ?$
6. $800 \times 900 = ?$
7. $9,000 - 8,000 = ?$
8. $9,000 - 800 = ?$
9. $9,000 - 80 = ?$
10. $9,000,000 - 8 = ?$

TUESDAY *Prime Numbers*

Write Yes or No.

1. 15
2. 16
3. 17
4. 18
5. 19
6. 20
7. 21
8. 22
9. 23
10. 24

WEDNESDAY *How Much Are?*

1. 20 quarters in dollars?
2. 24 half-dollars in dollars?
3. 2 gallons of gas at $1.09 per gallon?
4. 3 quarts of milk at 99¢ per quart?
5. 5 hamburgers at $1.10 per hamburger?
6. 4 pounds of beef at $1.50 per pound?
7. 2 pair of shoes at $45 a pair?
8. 2 video games at $49 a game?
9. 2 bikes at $199 per bike?
10. 2 trucks at $15,000 per truck?

THURSDAY *Fractions and Percents*

Fractions and percents are both used to identify numbers less than 1. $1/2$ and $50/100$ and .50 all mean half of 1, and 50% means 50 out of 100. Our money system uses all of these fractions. Now it's time to relate all of them while using math.

1. $1/2 = 50/100 = $ ___%.
2. $1/4 = 25/100 = $ ___%.
3. $1/5 = 20/100 = $ ___%.
4. $1/10 = 10/100 = $ ___%.
5. $2/10 = 20/100 = $ ___%.
6. $3/10 = 30/100 = $ ___%.
7. $4/10 = 40/100 = $ ___%.
8. $5/10 = 50/100 = $ ___%.
9. $7/10 = 70/100 = $ ___%.
10. $9/10 = 90/100 = $ ___%.

FRIDAY *What Am I?*

1. A 90-degree or L-shaped angle.
2. A perfectly round geometric figure.
3. A geometric figure with 3 sides.
4. The distance from the center of a circle to its edge.
5. 2 straight lines that never intersect.
6. 2^3 (or $2 \times 2 \times 2 = $ ___).
7. The geometric name for the shape of a baseball or a soccer ball.
8. If *ova* means egg in Latin, what shape is an ovoid?
9. Most ice comes in this shape from your refrigerator's ice trays.
10. Most ice cream is put on this geometric shape.

Week 35 Questions

MONDAY *Prime Numbers*
Write Yes or No.

1. 43
2. 47
3. 49
4. 51
5. 53
6. 57
7. 61
8. 67
9. 71
10. 79

TUESDAY *Percents*

1. 50% of $100 = ?
2. 25% of $100 = ?
3. 10% of $100 = ?
4. 50% of $50 = ?
5. 10% of $20 = ?
6. 25% of $40 = ?
7. 50% of $30 = ?
8. 10% of $10 = ?
9. 20% of $100 = ?
10. 33% of $300 = ?

WEDNESDAY *Geometry and Measurement*
Write True or False.

1. $4/8$ is the same amount as $1/2$.
2. 100 meters is $1/10$ of a kilometer.
3. 3^2 is less than $1/2$ of 18 .
4. 30 days = 6 weeks.
5. 5 quarters are more than 30 nickels.
6. A pentagon has six sides.
7. A tricycle has 5 wheels.
8. $2 1/2$ feet = 30 inches.
9. A mile is longer than a kilometer.
10. A quart is more than a liter.

THURSDAY *Geometry and Measurement*
Write True or False.

1. An equilateral triangle has 4 equal sides.
2. A square has 4 equal sides.
3. Parallel lines intersect.
4. A rectangle has 5 right angles.
5. A triangle can have 2 right angles.
6. A half inch is larger than a centimeter.
7. A kilogram weighs a bit more than 2 pounds.
8. If you multiply by 0, the answer is always 0.
9. If you add 0 to a number, the answer is always 0.
10. If you subtract 0 from a number, the answer always remains the amount you started with.

FRIDAY *Who Am I?*

1. An L-shaped angle.
2. A figure with 4 equal sides and 4 right angles.
3. Two straight lines that run in the same direction and never intersect.
4. A straight line from the center of a circle to its edge.
5. 36 inches.
6. 365 days.
7. 2,000 pounds.
8. 32 fluid ounces.
9. 100 years.
10. The fourth Thursday of November.

Week 36 Questions

MONDAY *Fractions of All Kinds*

1. $2 \frac{1}{2} - 2 \frac{1}{4} = ?$
2. $5 \frac{1}{2} + 4 \frac{1}{2} = ?$
3. $3 \times \frac{1}{2} = ?$
4. One-half of a day = ? hours.
5. One-third of an hour = ? minutes.
6. One-fourth of a year = ? months.
7. $\frac{1}{2} - \frac{1}{4} = ?$
8. $\frac{3}{4} + \frac{2}{4} = ?$
9. $\frac{1}{2} + \frac{3}{4} = ?$
10. $\frac{1}{10}$ of an hour = ? minutes.

TUESDAY *Percents*

1. 10% of $55 = ?
2. 10% of $25 = ?
3. 25% of $400 = ?
4. 50% of $1.00 = ?
5. 10% of $300 = ?
6. 50% of $5.00 = ?
7. 25% of $1,000 = ?
8. 25% of $44 = ?
9. 75% of $44 = ?
10. 90% of $100 = ?

WEDNESDAY *Geometry and Measurement*
Write True or False.

1. $\frac{6}{12}$ is the same amount as $\frac{1}{2}$.
2. 100 meters = 1 kilometer.
3. (3 x 3) is equal to (5 x 5) - (4 x 4).
4. 30 days = 5 weeks.
5. 5 quarters are more than 20 nickels.
6. A pentagon has six sides.
7. A tricycle has 4 wheels.
8. 3 feet = 30 inches.
9. A kilometer is longer than a mile.
10. A quart is more than a liter.

THURSDAY *Geometry and Measurement*
Write True or False.

1. All triangles have 3 equal sides.
2. A square always has 4 equal sides.
3. Parallel lines never intersect.
4. A rectangle always has 4 right angles.
5. A triangle can have only one right angle.
6. An inch is about $2 \frac{1}{2}$ centimeters.
7. A pound weighs about $\frac{1}{2}$ of a kilogram.
8. If you multiply by 1, the answer is always the same amount you started with.
9. If you add 1, the answer is always 1 larger.
10. If you divide by 1, the answer is always the amount you started with.

FRIDAY *Who Am I?*

1. A 120° angle.
2. A figure with 3 equal sides and 3 equal angles.
3. Two straight lines that cross.
4. A straight line that runs from the edge of a circle through its center to its opposite edge.
5. 5,280 feet.
6. 366 days.
7. 1,000 kilograms.
8. 4 quarts.
9. 10 years.
10. The day after December 31st.

Week 37 Questions

MONDAY *Squaring and Cubing*

1. $2 \times 2 \times 2$ is 2^3. How much is 2^3?
2. How much is $3 \times 3 \times 3$ or 3^3?
3. How much is 5^3?
4. How much is 10^3?
5. How much is $10^3 - 10^2$?
6. How much is $5^3 - 5^2$?
7. How much is $2^2 + 2^3$?
8. Which is larger, 2^3 or 3^2?
9. Which is less, 5^3 or 10^2?
10. What is $10^3 \times 10^3$?

TUESDAY *Half of. . .*

1. Half of 3 = ?
2. Half of 50 = ?
3. Half of 120 = ?
4. Half of 2,400 = ?
5. Half of 30,000 = ?
6. Half of 140,000 = ?
7. Half of 2,400,000 = ?
8. Half of 50,000,00 = ?
9. Half of 800,000,000 = ?
10. Half of 1,000,000,000 = ?

WEDNESDAY *How Many?*

1. How many sides on an octagon?
2. How many sides on a triangle?
3. How many faces on a square-based pyramid?
4. How many quarts in a gallon?
5. How many pints in a quart?
6. How many cups in a pint?
7. How many feet in a mile?
8. How many weeks in a year?
9. How many nickels in a dollar?
10. How many pennies in a $5 bill?

THURSDAY *Money Problems*

1. Mike has $5. Will he be able to buy 3 sandwiches at $1.60 each?
2. Michelle has $10. Will she be able to buy 4 ink pens at $2.50 each?
3. Melvin has $14. Can he buy 2 movie tickets at $7.50 each?
4. Melissa has $20. Can she buy 3 pairs of socks at $6.50 each?
5. Mario has $25. Can he buy 3 airplane models at $8.50 each?
6. Marion has $30. Can she buy 4 scarves at $7.50 each?
7. Steven has $35. Can he afford a $19 shirt and $16 shorts?
8. Stephanie has $40. Can she buy 3 blouses at $13.50 each?
9. John has $50. Can he buy a $15 hat and 12 golf balls at $3 each?
10. Johnnette has $75. Can she buy 4 new CDs at $18 per CD?

FRIDAY *Geometry Review*

Write True or False.

1. An open figure is not completely closed.
2. A symmetric figure can be folded in half to make identical parts.
3. Perpendicular lines are parallel to each other.
4. A square can also be called a rectangle.
5. The distance around a figure is called a perimeter.
6. A polygon is a circular figure.
7. Any closed figure that lies on a flat surface is called a plane figure.
8. Similar figures must be the same size.
9. Parallel lines cross each other.
10. Congruent figures have the same size and shape.

Week 38 Questions

MONDAY *Squaring and Cubing*

1. How much is $3^2 - 2^3$?
2. How much is $3^3 - 3$?
3. How much is $5^3 - 5$?
4. How much is 10^3?
5. How much is $10^3 + 10^2 + 10$?
6. How much is $5^3 + 5^2$?
7. How much is $2^3 + 2^3$
8. Which is larger, 3^3 or 5^2?
9. Which is less, 5^3 or 120?
10. What is $10 \times 10^2 \times 10^3$?

TUESDAY *Third of...*

1. A third of 30 = ?
2. A third of 90 = ?
3. A third of 120 = ?
4. A third of 333 = ?
5. A third of 360 = ?
6. A third of 6,000 = ?
7. A third of 90,000 = ?
8. A third of 333,333 = ?
9. A third of 9,999,999 = ?
10. A third of 3,000,000,000 = ?

WEDNESDAY *How Many?*

1. How many months in a season?
2. How many seasons in a year?
3. How many cups make a pint?
4. How many cups in a quart?
5. How many decades in a century?
6. How many centuries in a millennium?
7. How many hours in a day?
8. How many days in October?
9. How many weeks in a season?
10. How many seconds in an hour?

THURSDAY *Correct Change*

1. What is the change from $5 after spending $2.51?
2. What is the change from $10 after spending $6.75?
3. What is the change from $15 after spending $12.25?
4. What is the change from $20 after spending $19.20?
5. What is the change from $25 after spending $23.80?
6. What is the change from $30 after spending $26.20?
7. What is the change from $40 after spending $35.55?
8. What is the change from a $50 bill after spending $27.50?
9. What is the change from a $100 bill after spending $86.99?
10. What is the change from a $100 bill after spending $93.10?

FRIDAY *Geometry Review*
Write True or False.

1. Intersecting lines never cross.
2. A diameter is a line that runs from the center of a circle to the outer circle.
3. A corner is when 2 sides meet.
4. An acute angle is more than 90 degrees.
5. The base is the bottom of a figure.
6. A degree is a unit to measure angles.
7. An obtuse angle is less than 90 degrees.
8. A rectangle has 4 square corners.
9. A rhombus looks like a square pushed over to look like a diamond.
10. An equilateral triangle has 3 equal angles.

Week 39 Questions

MONDAY *Measurement*
Write True or False.

1. A square has 4 right angles.
2. A clockface can be divided into 4 right angles.
3. A triangle can have 2 right angles.
4. A rectangle has 6 right angles.
5. Parallel lines never intersect.
6. February has 30 days in a leap year.
7. 2 quarts make a half gallon.
8. 1 meter is longer than 1 yard.
9. A centimeter longer than an inch.
10. A kilometer is longer than a mile.

TUESDAY *Fraction Problems*

1. $5/2$ = what mixed number?
2. $7/3$ = what mixed number?
3. $9/4$ = what mixed number?
4. Which is larger: $1/2$ or $1/10$?
5. Which is larger: $1/4$ or $1/5$?
6. Which is larger: $3/10$ or $1/2$?
7. $1/2 + 1/4 + 1/8 = ?$
8. $5/8 + 5/8$ = what mixed number?
9. $3/7 + 5/7$ = what mixed number?
10. $1/3 + 1/3 + 1/3$ = what whole number?

WEDNESDAY *Fraction Operations*

1. $1 - 2/3 = ?$
2. $2 - 1/2 = ?$
3. $10 - 1\,1/2 = ?$
4. $10 - 9\,1/2 = ?$
5. $10 - 5\,1/2 = ?$
6. $5\,1/2 + 5\,1/2 = ?$
7. $2\,1/2 + 4\,1/2 = ?$
8. $2\,1/2 + 1/2 = ?$
9. Double $2\,1/2$.
10. Triple $3\,1/3$.

THURSDAY *Math Terminology*
Write True or False.

1. A decimal point separates whole numbers from decimal numbers.
2. Compatible numbers are difficult to compute mentally.
3. Digits are the math symbols 0 to 9.
4. Inverse operations are the same.
5. A product is an addition answer.
6. Square numbers are numbers in squares.
7. A divisor is the number that is divided.
8. Remainders are what's left from addition.
9. The numerator is the top number of a fraction.
10. The denominator is the bottom number of a fraction.

FRIDAY *Geometry Quiz*

1. If one side of a square is 4 inches, how long are the other sides?
2. If one side of a rectangle is 10 cm., how long is the opposite side?
3. If one side of an equilateral triangle is 25 centimeters, how long are the other sides?
4. If one side of a square is 3 inches, how much is its perimeter?
5. If one side of an equilateral triangle is 5 centimeters, how much is its perimeter?
6. How many sides on an octagon?
7. How many sides on a pentagon?
8. How many sides on a hexagon?
9. How many sides on a circle?
10. How many semicircles make a circle?

Week 40 Questions

MONDAY *Terminology*
Write True or False.

1. Equivalent fractions have different numbers, but equal the same amount.
2. Unlike fractions have different numerators.
3. Mixed numbers are numbers that are mixed up.
4. Percent means a number in relationship to 100.
5. A cylinder has 2 congruent circles.
6. A triangular pyramid has 4 faces.
7. A rectangular pyramid has 5 faces.
8. An octangular pyramid has 8 faces.
9. A sphere is a flat object like a circle.
10. A cube is made of 6 identical squares.

TUESDAY *Fraction Problems*

1. $5/4$ = what mixed number?
2. $6/3$ = what number?
3. $13/4$ = what mixed number?
4. Which is larger: $1/3$ or $3/4$?
5. Which is larger: $3/4$ or $3/2$?
6. Which is larger: $5/12$ or $1/2$?
7. $1/2 + 3/2$ = ?
8. $2/4 + 3/4$ = what mixed number?
9. $3/5 + 4/5$ = what mixed number?
10. $2/3 + 2/3 + 2/3$ = what whole number?

WEDNESDAY *Fraction Operations*

1. $2 - 2/3$ = ?
2. $6 - 1/2$ = ?
3. $10 - 7 1/2$ =?
4. $20 - 9 1/2$ = ?
5. $12 - 5 1/2$ = ?
6. $5 1/4 + 5 3/4$ = ?
7. $2 1/3 + 4 2/3$ = ?
8. $21 1/4 + 3/4$ = ?
9. Double $12 1/2$.
10. Triple $10 1/3$.

THURSDAY *Geometry and Measurement*
Write True or False.

1. A rhombus has no right angles.
2. A circle can be divided into 4 right angles.
3. A triangle can have 3 right angles.
4. A pentagon has 5 right angles.
5. Parallel lines eventually intersect.
6. February has 28 days in a leap year.
7. 3 quarts equal $3/4$ of a gallon.
8. 100 meters are longer than 100 yards.
9. A centimeter is about the width of your small fingernail.
10. Driving 60 kilometers per hour is faster than driving 60 miles per hour.

FRIDAY *Geometry Quiz*

1. If one side of a square is 10 inches, how many of the other sides are that long?
2. If one side of a parallelogram is 4 inches, how long is the opposite side?
3. If one side of an equilateral triangle is 3 centimeters long, are both of the other sides that long?
4. If one side of a square is 12 inches, what is its perimeter?
5. If one side of an equilateral triangle is 30 centimeters, how much is its perimeter?
6. What is the name of an 8-sided figure?
7. What is the name of a 5-sided figure?
8. What is the name of a 6-sided figure?
9. A circle has how many sides?
10. A semicircle is what fraction of a circle?

Week 41 Questions

MONDAY *Multiply and Divide*

1. 100 x 532 = ?
2. 1,000 x 345 = ?
3. 500,000 ÷ 1,000 = ?
4. 440 ÷ 10 = ?
5. 10 x 750,000 = ?
6. 7,500,000 ÷ 10 = ?
7. 1,000 x 500 = ?
8. 70,000 ÷ 10,000 = ?
9. 1,000 x 1,000 = ?
10. 1,000,000 ÷ 1,000 = ?

TUESDAY *Fraction Action*

1. Write $2 \frac{1}{4}$ as an improper fraction.
2. Write $3 \frac{1}{3}$ as an improper fraction.
3. Write $10 \frac{1}{2}$ as an improper fraction.
4. Write $\frac{9}{4}$ as a mixed number.
5. Write $\frac{15}{10}$ as a mixed number.
6. Write $\frac{50}{2}$ as a regular number.
7. Double $12 \frac{1}{2}$.
8. Triple $3 \frac{1}{4}$.
9. Quadruple $10 \frac{1}{4}$.
10. What is 10 times $2 \frac{1}{2}$?

WEDNESDAY *Percents & Fractions*

Write True or False.

1. 75% = three-fourths.
2. 50% = one-half
3. 10% = one-tenth
4. 25% = one-fifth
5. 30% = three-tenths
6. 40% = two-fifths
7. 60% = three-fifths
8. 80% = four-fifths
9. 90% = nine-tenths
10. 99% = ninety nine-one hundredths

THURSDAY *Weight & Height*

1. May weighs 80 pounds. Her dog weighs half her weight. What is its weight?
2. Ben weighs 180 pounds. His dog is half his weight. What is its weight?
3. Abbie weighs 3 times her dog's 40 pounds. What is Abbie's weight?
4. Cindy weighs 100 pounds. Her cat weighs $\frac{1}{4}$ that. How heavy is it?
5. Olaf is 4'9" tall. How many inches tall is he?
6. Dawn is 5'5" tall. How many inches must she grow to be 6'2"?
7. A giraffe is 15-feet tall. How much is that in inches?
8. An Amazon snake is 20 feet long. How much is that in inches?
9. A baby elephant weighs a half ton. What is that in pounds?
10. How many inches in $10 \frac{1}{2}$ feet?

FRIDAY *Fractions of . . .*

1. $\frac{1}{2}$ of a thousand = ?
2. $\frac{1}{4}$ of a hundred = ?
3. $\frac{3}{4}$ of a thousand = ?
4. $\frac{1}{10}$ of a thousand = ?
5. $\frac{3}{10}$ of a thousand = ?
6. $\frac{1}{2}$ hour + $\frac{1}{4}$ hour = ? minutes.
7. $\frac{1}{2}$ hour + $\frac{1}{10}$ hour = ? minutes
8. $\frac{3}{10}$ of a century + $\frac{6}{10}$ century equal how many years?
9. $\frac{1}{2}$ of a millennium equals how many years?
10. A hundred years - $\frac{1}{10}$ of a century equal how many years?

Week 42 Questions

MONDAY *Geometry Quiz*
Write True or False.

1. An acute angle is less than 90°.
2. An obtuse angle is greater than 90°.
3. A triangular-based prism has 5 faces.
4. A cube is made of 6 square faces.
5. A square-based pyramid has 5 faces.
6. A triangular prism is made of 2 triangles and 3 rectangles.
7. A rectangular prism has 6 sides.
8. An isosceles triangle has 2 equal sides.
9. An equilateral triangle has 3 equal sides.
10. An equilateral triangle has 3 right angles.

TUESDAY *Fraction Warm Up*

1. Write $9/10$ as a decimal.
2. Write $9/100$ as a decimal.
3. $1/4$ of 36 = ?
4. $1/2$ of 15 =?
5. $1/2$ of 300 = ?
6. $4/5$ of a dollar = ? cents
7. $3/4$ of a kg. = ? grams
8. $1/2$ of a liter = ? milliliters
9. $1/4$ of a minute = ? seconds
10. $1/3$ of a day = ? hours

WEDNESDAY *Fractions to Decimals*

1. Write $1/2$ as a decimal.
2. Write $1/3$ as a decimal.
3. Write $1/4$ as a decimal.
4. Write $1/5$ as a decimal.
5. Write $1/10$ as a decimal.
6. Write $4/10$ as a decimal.
7. Write $3/10$ as a decimal.
8. Write $3/4$ as a decimal.
9. Write $3/5$ as a decimal.
10. Write $2/3$ as a decimal.

THURSDAY *Polygon Multiplication*

1. How many sides on 6 hexagons?
2. How many sides on 8 octagons?
3. How many sides on 5 pentagons?
4. How many sides on 3 triangles?
5. How many sides on 4 rectangles?
6. How many sides on 7 heptagons?
7. How many sides on 9 nonagons?
8. How many sides on 10 decagons?
9. How many sides on 20 dodecagons?
10. A trapezoid and a rhombus = ? sides.

FRIDAY *Which Is Greater?*

1. 10 dollars or 90 dimes?
2. 10 quarters or 30 dimes?
3. 400 pennies or 10 half-dollars?
4. 20 nickels or 5 quarters?
5. Ten $5 bills or a $100 bill?
6. 3,000 pounds or a ton?
7. 3 quarts or a gallon?
8. 10 inches or a foot?
9. 5 feet or 2 yards?
10. 150 minutes or 3 hours?

Week 43 Questions

MONDAY *Warm Up*

1. What are the two factors of 35 ?
2. What is the product of 20 and 30 ?
3. The square root of 36 = ?
4. $3/10$ of 100 = ?
5. 9^2 = ?
6. 2,000 + 600 + 4 = ?
7. 2 x 5 x 30 = ?
8. Write $3\ 2/3$ as an improper fraction.
9. $1/2 - 4/10$ = ?
10. 50% of $20 = ?

TUESDAY *Averages*

To find an average, add the numbers given & divide their sum by the amount of numbers. For example, 10 + 2 + 8 = 30. Then divide 30 by 3. The average is 10.

1. What's the average of 15, 10, & 20 ?
2. What's the average of 20, 25, & 15 ?
3. What's the average of 7, 8 & 12 ?
4. What's the average of 30, 50 & 19 ?
5. What's the average of 25, 40, & 10 ?
6. What's the average of 22, 33, & 5 ?
7. What's the average of 10, 45, & 5 ?
8. What's the average of 24, 36, & 15 ?
9. What's the average of 19, 21, & 5 ?
10. What's the average of 8, 52, & 30 ?

WEDNESDAY *Adding Fractions*

1. $3/4 + 3/4$ = ?
2. $2/5 + 3/5$ = ?
3. $2\ 3/4 + 2\ 3/4$ = ?
4. $3\ 1/2 + 5\ 1/4$ = ?
5. $4\ 1/4 + 3/4$ = ?
6. $10\ 2/5 + 11\ 3/5$ = ?
7. $25\ 3/5 + 25\ 2/5$ = ?
8. $3\ 1/2 + 5/10$ = ?
9. $6\ 4/5 + 6\ 2/5$ = ?
10. $1\ 1/2 + 1\ 1/2 + 1\ 1/2$ = ?

THURSDAY *Squares*

1. 10^2 x 9 = ?
2. $3^2 + 4^2 = ?^2$
3. $10^2 - 0^2 = ?^2$
4. $2^2 + 4^2$ = ?
5. $3^2 + 2^3$ = ?
6. $10^3 + 10^2$ = ?
7. $10^3 - 10^2$ = ?
8. $5^2 - 1^2$ = ? dozen
9. 4 dozen + 1 = $?^2$
10. $1/2$ of $10^2 = ?^2 + 1$

FRIDAY *Geometry*

1. If the radius of a circle is 6 inches, how long is its diameter?
2. What's the perimeter of an equilateral triangle whose sides are each 5 inches?
3. What's the perimeter of an equilateral pentagon whose sides are 7 inches each?
4. How many square inches in a square whose sides are 6 inches each?
5. What's the square footage of a rectangular room whose dimensions are 10 ft. by 15 ft.?
6. The perimeter of a circle is pi (3.14) times its diameter (2 in.). Multiply to get its perimeter.
7. What is the perimeter of a circle with a diameter of 3 inches. (Multiply pi (3.14) times 3 inches.)
8. Calculate the perimeter of an equilateral hexagon whose sides are 10 inches each.
9. Calculate the perimeter of an equilateral octagon whose sides are 6 inches each.
10. Calculate the perimeter of an equilateral heptagon whose sides are 7 centimeters each.

Week 44 Questions

MONDAY *Warm Up*

1. Give the basic factors of 27.
2. What is the product of 200 and 300?
3. The difference between 800 & 720 is?
4. The square root of 64?
5. $3,000 + 20 + 8 = ?$
6. $5^3 = ?$
7. $10 \times 20 \times 5 = ?$
8. Write 7/3 as a mixed number.
9. $3 \frac{1}{2} + 5 \frac{4}{10} = ?$
10. 50% of $2,000 = ?

TUESDAY *Averages*

What's the average of:

1. ... 35, 15, and 10?
2. ... 21, 19, and 35?
3. ... 5, 7, and 12?
4. ... 50, 30, and 40?
5. ... 200, 600, and 100?
6. ... 10, 20, 30, and 40?
7. ... 5, 15, 25, and 35?
8. ... 20, 20, 35, and 5?
9. ... 300, 400, 100, and 200?
10. ... 150, 50, 120, and 80?

WEDNESDAY *Subtracting Fractions*

1. $2 \frac{1}{2} - 1 \frac{1}{4} = ?$
2. $1 \frac{7}{10} - \frac{3}{10} = ?$
3. $6 \frac{2}{3} - 4 \frac{2}{3} = ?$
4. $10 - 8 \frac{1}{2} = ?$
5. $4 - 3 \frac{3}{4} = ?$
6. $5 - \frac{2}{3} = ?$
7. $9 \frac{3}{5} - 7 = ?$
8. $3 \frac{1}{2} - \frac{5}{10} = ?$
9. $1 - \frac{1}{2} - \frac{1}{4} = ?$
10. $20 \frac{2}{3} - 10 \frac{1}{3} = ?$

THURSDAY *Super Squares*

1. $10^2 - 9 = ?$
2. $5^2 - 4^2 = ?^2$
3. $10^2 - 8^2 = ?^2$
4. $4^2 - 2^2 = ?$
5. $3^2 - 2^3 = ?$
6. $10^3 - 10^2 = ?$
7. $10^2 \times 10^3 = ?$
8. $6^2 = ?$ dozen
9. $8^2 - 2^2 = ?$
10. $\frac{1}{4}$ of $10^2 = ?^2$

FRIDAY *Geometry Formulas*

1. If the diameter of a circle is 6 inches, how long is its radius?
2. What's the perimeter of an equilateral pentagon whose sides are 2 ft.?
3. What's the perimeter of an equilateral hexagon whose sides are 5 inches?
4. What's the area of a rectangle whose sides are 5 feet by 3 feet?
5. What's the perimeter of a rectangle whose sides are 7 meters by 10 meters?
6. What's the area of a rectangle whose sides are 7 meters by 10 meters?
7. What is the circumference of a circle whose diameter is 5 inches times pi (3.14)?
8. What is the area of a circle with a radius of 2 cm?
   (Hint: pi times the radius squared)
9. The perimeter of an equilateral pentagon with 5 inch sides = ?
10. The perimeter of an equilateral decagon with 8 cm. sides = ?

Week 45 Questions

MONDAY *Warm Up*

1. What's the average of 3, 7, and 20?
2. What's the average of 14, 16, 30?
3. $(1/2$ of 200) + $(1/2$ of 8) = ?
4. $1/2$ of $1/2$ = ?
5. $1/2$ x 24 = ?
6. The square root of 49 is?
7. The square root of 100 is?
8. The square root of 400 is?
9. 10^4 = ?
10. 100^2 = ?

TUESDAY *Introduction to Range*

The range of a group of numbers is the difference between the largest and smallest numbers in the group. Give the range for the following numbers. (Write the numbers on the board.)

1. 7, 8, 9, 10,
2. 12, 15, 18, 20
3. 6, 9, 5, 7
4. 33, 22, 55, 44
5. 40, 45, 35, 30
6. 5/10, 3/10, 2/10, 7/10
7. 33%, 35%, 40%, 42%
8. 23.8, 24.1, 24.5, 24.8
9. 11.2, 12.0, 12.4, 11.8
10. 123, 132, 126, 129

WEDNESDAY *Division of Fractions*

Divide the whole number first. Then divide the numerator of the fraction.

1. $3/2$ divided by 3 = ?
2. $3/4$ divided by 3 = ?
3. $6/10$ divided by 3 = ?
4. $2/3$ divided by 2 = ?
5. $2 \, 2/5$ divided by 2 = ?
6. $3 \, 3/4$ divided by 3 = ?
7. $5 \, 5/10$ divided by 5 = ?
8. $9 \, 9/10$ divided by 9 = ?
9. $6/8$ divided by 2 = ?
10. $12 \, 3/4$ divided by 3 = ?

THURSDAY *Fractions and Percents*

Write True or False.

1. 75% is the equivalent of $3/4$.
2. .20 is the equivalent of $2/10$.
3. $4/5$ is the equivalent of .80.
4. .7 is the equivalent of 70%.
5. $1/5$ is the equivalent of 20%.
6. $2/3$ is the equivalent of 60%.
7. $1/6$ is the equivalent of $16 \, 2/3$ %.
8. $1/3$ is the equivalent of $33 \, 1/3$ %.
9. 40% is the equivalent of $2/5$.
10. $14 \, 2/7$ % is the equivalent of $1/7$.

FRIDAY *Geometry Guess—Who Am I?*

1. I am an equilateral rectangle.
2. I am half a diameter.
3. I am 90° and L-shaped.
4. I am 360° and perfectly round.
5. I am an angle wider than 90°.
6. I am an angle less than 90°.
7. I am a closed figure with 10 sides.
8. I am a closed figure with 8 sides.
9. I am the 3-dimensional version of a square. I have 6 faces.
10. I am the 3-dimensional version of a circle.

Week 46 Questions

MONDAY *Integers*

Integers are more than regular numbers. They include both positive and negative numbers. With integers, you can add and subtract positive and negative numbers. However, if you subtract a negative number, it becomes a positive number: 2 negatives make a positive. Put these on the board:
$2 - (-2) = 4$ and $-5 + 3 = -2$

1. $-7 + 3 = ?$
2. $-6 - 8 = ?$
3. $9 + (-11) = ?$
4. $-9 + (-11) = ?$
5. $-4 + (-20) = ?$
6. $5 - (-12) = ?$
7. $8 - (+12) = ?$
8. $-12 + 20 = ?$
9. $23 - (-40) = ?$
10. $18 - (+30) = ?$

TUESDAY *Introduction to Mode*

The mode of a group of numbers is the number that occurs most often. There may be more than one mode or none depending on the numbers.
What's the mode(s) in each group of numbers? (Write the numbers on the board.)

1. 7, 8, 4, 5, 5, 2
2. 34, 35, 37, 35, 32
3. 12, 13, 15, 13, 11
4. 54, 56, 57, 55, 54
5. 76, 80, 78, 77, 78
6. 99, 101, 102, 101
7. 345, 346, 342, 345
8. 689, 679, 687, 671
9. $7 \frac{1}{2}$, $7 \frac{1}{3}$, $7 \frac{1}{4}$, $7 \frac{1}{2}$
10. 3.8, 3.9, 3.9, 3.7, 3.8

WEDNESDAY *Review Relationships*

1. 65 millimeters = ? centimeters
2. 18 inches = what fraction of a foot
3. 60 hours = ? days
4. 500 pounds = what fraction of a ton
5. 7 quarts = what fraction of 2 gallons
6. 125 centimeters = what % of a meter
7. 5 days is what fraction of a week?
8. 150% of a meter = ? centimeters
9. 25% of a foot = ? inches
10. 50% of $50 = ? dollars

THURSDAY *Which Is More?*

1. $\frac{3}{4}$ of a dozen *or* 10?
2. 33 *or* $2 \frac{1}{2}$ dozen?
3. 9 x 9 *or* 4 x 21?
4. 6 x 9 *or* 72?
5. $125 *or* 6 $20 bills?
6. 3 pounds *or* 2 kilograms?
7. 2 quarts *or* 2 liters?
8. 4 weeks *or* the month of May?
9. 3 minutes *or* 200 seconds?
10. 48 hours *or* 3 days?

FRIDAY *Remembering Our Roots*

1. What is the square root of 25?
2. What is the square root of 49?
3. What is the square root of 36?
4. What is the square root of 16?
5. What is the square root of 81?
6. What is the square root of 64?
7. What is the square root of 9?
8. What is the square root of 100?
9. What is the square root of 121?
10. What is the square root of 144?

Week 47 Questions

MONDAY *Warm Up*

1. (10 x 25) + (8 x 25) = ?
2. 26, 24, 27, 22 —What's the range?
3. $.50, $.75, $.60 —What's the range?
4. 8, 6, 7, 5, 8 —What's the mode?
5. $25, $30, $27, $19 —What's the mode?
6. 45, 44, 44, 46, 45 —What's the mode?
7. -5 + 135 = ?
8. -5 x (-30) = ?
9. 16 - (-14) ÷ 2 = ?
10. -7 + 3 + (-10) = ?

TUESDAY *Introduction to Median*

The middle number of an ordered series of numbers is called the median. If you had the numbers 3, 4, 6, 10, 11, the number 6 would be median. What's the median for the following groups of numbers? (Write the numbers on the board.)

1. 2, 4, 6, 7, 9
2. 15, 25, 35, 45, 55
3. 34, 36, 38, 40, 42
4. 200, 300, 400
5. 200, 300, 400, 500, 600
6. $5, $7, $11, $13, $25
7. $\frac{1}{4}$, $\frac{1}{3}$, $\frac{1}{2}$, $\frac{2}{3}$, $\frac{3}{4}$
8. $\frac{1}{5}$, $\frac{2}{5}$, $\frac{3}{5}$, $\frac{4}{5}$, $\frac{5}{5}$
9. 23%, 27%, 33%
10. 6.5, 7.6, 8.7, 9.8, 10.9

WEDNESDAY *Square Roots*

1. What is the square root of 1?
2. What is the square root of 9?
3. What is the square root of 25?
4. What is the square root of 49?
5. What is the square root of 81?
6. What is the square root of 121?
7. What is the square root of 400?
8. What is the square root of 1,600?
9. What is the square root of 3,600?
10. What is the square root of 8,100?

THURSDAY *Degrees*

1. If a compass has 360 degrees, how many degrees between north & south?
2. If a compass has 360 degrees, how many degrees between north & east?
3. If a compass has 360 degrees, how many degrees between north & west?
4. What are the degrees of a square angle?
5. What are the degrees of each angle of an equilateral triangle?
6. If a triangle has a right angle, how many degrees do the other 2 angles together?
7. If a triangle has an obtuse angle of 120 degrees, what is the sum of the other two angles?
8. If a triangle has an acute angle of 30 degrees, what will be the sum of the other 2 angles?
9. If an isosceles triangle has two 70 degree angles at its base, what are the degrees of the other angle?
10. If a parallelogram has two 60 degree opposite angles, what are the degrees of each of the other 2 angles?

FRIDAY *Elementary Algebra*

Algebra is a branch of mathematics in which quantities (numbers) are expressed as letters. Problems are solved in the form of equations using various possible numbers. For example, x + y = 10. One solution would be 3 + 7 = 10. However, another solution could be 4 + 6 = 10. Let's start with x + y = 10 (put on the board). Using the equation x + y = 10:

1. If x = 2, what must y be?
2. If x = 3, what must y be?
3. If x = 4, what must y be?
4. If x = 9, what must y be?
5. If x = 10, what must y be?
6. If x = 7 $\frac{1}{2}$, what must y be?
7. If x = 9 $\frac{1}{2}$, what must y be?
8. If x = 2.5, what must y be?
9. If x = 9.9, what must y be?
10. If x = 0, what must y be?

Week 48 Questions

MONDAY *Warm Up*
(Write the numbers on the board.)

1. 33, 37, 42, 50—What's the range?
2. 12, 14, 13, 14, 10—What's the mode?
3. 10, 12, 15, 18, 20—What's the median?
4. 120, 115, 110, 105—What's the range?
5. 3.2, 3.4, 3.5, 3.8—What's the mode?
6. 44, 45, 47, 50, 55—What's the median?
7. 2, 4, 5, 4, 2—What's the mode?
8. If x = 5, what must y be to equal 15?
9. If x = 12, what must y be to equal 15?
10. If x = 9 $\frac{1}{2}$, what must y be to equal 15?

TUESDAY *Fractions of . . .*

1. $\frac{1}{3}$ of a leap year = ? days.
2. $\frac{1}{4}$ of a century = ? years.
3. $\frac{1}{5}$ of a millennium = ? years.
4. $\frac{1}{6}$ of a leap year = ? months
5. $\frac{1}{3}$ of a minute = ? seconds.
6. $\frac{9}{10}$ of an hour = ? minutes.
7. $\frac{3}{4}$ of a liter = ? milliliters.
8. $\frac{3}{4}$ of a day = ? hours.
9. $\frac{1}{10}$ of a yardstick = ? inches.
10. $\frac{1}{10}$ of a ton = ? pounds.

WEDNESDAY *More Algebra*
To solve the equation x - y = 10 (put the equation on the board):

1. If x = 20, what must y be?
2. If x = 15, what must y be?
3. If x = 30, what must y be?
4. If x = 50, what must y be?
5. If x = 10, what must y be?
6. If x = 100, what must y be?
7. If x = 300, what must y be?
8. If x = 500, what must y be?
9. If x = 10 $\frac{1}{2}$, what must y be?
10. If x = 37 $\frac{1}{2}$, what must y be?

THURSDAY *Introduction to the Mean*
The mean is the sum of the numbers in the group divided by the amount of the numbers in the group to get an average of the group. For example, 7 + 8 + 10 = 36 divided by 3 = 12.
(Write the numbers on the board.)

1. Find the mean of 10, 2, and 21.
2. Find the mean of 5, 6, 8, and 9.
3. Find the mean of 20, 30, and 70.
4. Find the mean of 200, 300, and 1,000.
5. Find the mean of 3, 5, 8, 10, and 14.
6. Find the mean of 12, 14, 16, and 18.
7. Find the mean of 3, 5, 6, and 10.
8. Find the mean of 20, 30, and 100.
9. Find the mean of 4,000, 7,000, and 10,000.
10. Find the mean of 1, 2, 3, 4, 5, 6, and 7.

FRIDAY *Ratio*
A ratio is a comparison of two numbers. It's similar to how many times a number is greater than another number. For example, a dollar is 100 times larger than a penny. It is expressed this way —100: 1 (on the board). Use this way to show the ratios of the following problems.

1. The ratio of a foot to an inch is?
2. The ratio of a yard to a foot is?
3. The ratio of a minute to a second is?
4. The ratio of a week to a day is?
5. The ratio of a year to a day is?
6. The ratio of a gallon to a quart is?
7. The ratio of a dollar to a nickel is?
8. The ratio of a ton to a pound is?
9. The ratio of the alphabet to one letter is?
10. The ratio of Roman numeral C to numeral L is?

Week 49 Questions

MONDAY *Warm Up*

1. 15, 15, 20, 25, 35—What's the range?
2. 15, 15, 20, 25, 35—What's the mode?
3. 15, 15, 20, 25, 35—What's the median?
4. 15, 15, 20, 25, 35—What's the mean?
5. $-6 + 8 = ?$
6. $-10 - 14 = ?$
7. $6 + (-7) = ?$
8. $-12 - (-15) = ?$
9. $25 - (-30) = ?$
10. $-100 + 45 = ?$

TUESDAY *Halves & Ratios*

1. $4 \frac{1}{2}$ hours work at $50 per hour = ?
2. $3 \frac{1}{2}$ yards of cloth at $5 per yard = ?
3. $5 \frac{1}{2}$ gallons = ? quarts.
4. $6 \frac{1}{2}$ tons = ? pounds.
5. $8 \frac{1}{2}$ meters = ? centimeters.
6. The ratio of a mile to a foot is . . .
7. The ratio of a gallon to a pint is . . .
8. The ratio of $50 to a dime is . . .
9. The ratio of the 100% to 2% is . . .
10. The ratio of the alphabet to one letter?

WEDNESDAY *Algebra*

Put on the board: x = 5   y = 6
Solve the equations:

1. $2x + y = ?$
2. $x - y = ?$
3. $8x - 5y = ?$
4. $20x - 50 - 5y = ?$
5. $x^2 - 4y = ?$
6. $6x \div y = ?$
7. $7x - y^2 = ?$
8. $20x - 64 - y^2 = ?$
9. $x + x^2 = ?$
10. $xy = ?$

THURSDAY *True or False?*

1. $\frac{7}{10}$ is larger than $\frac{3}{4}$.
2. A hexagon has 2 more sides than an octagon.
3. 6 decades = 600 years
4. 6 hours = 300 minutes
5. $2.5 + 3.8$ is larger than 6.
6. A cylinder is the shape of an oval.
7. A parallelogram has opposite parallel sides.
8. Both a square and a rectangle have 4 sides.
9. A pentagon has 4 more sides than a triangle.
10. A trillion is written with 5 commas.

FRIDAY *Patterns*

What's the next number?

1. 10, 20, 40, 80, 160, ___?
2. 3, 9, 27, 81, ___?
3. 4, 9, 16, 25, 36, 49, ___?
4. 5, 25, 125, ___?
5. 4, 7, 14, 17, 24, 27, ___?
6. 7; 77; 777; 7,777; ___?
7. 1,000,001; 100,001; 10,001; ___?
8. 123, 234, 345, 456, ___?
9. 13, 26, 52, 104, ___?
10. 45; 450; 4,500; 45,000; 450,000; ___?

Week 50 Questions

MONDAY *Find the Factors*
Break down the numbers to their smallest factors.
For instance, 12 is made up of 3 x 2 x 2.

1. 10
2. 21
3. 22
4. 24
5. 25
6. 27
7. 30
8. 33
9. 36
10. 40

TUESDAY *Ratios and Fractions*
Put on the board —The ratio of 1 to $1/5$ is 5:1.

1. The ratio of 1 to $1/3$ is?
2. The ratio of 2 to $1/3$ is?
3. The ratio of 5 to $1/4$ is?
4. The ratio of 6 to $1/2$ is?
5. The ratio of 10 to $1/3$ is?
6. The ratio of 20 to $1/2$ is?
7. The ratio of 30 to $1/3$ is?
8. The ratio of 50 to $1/2$ is?
9. The ratio of 100 to $1/4$ is?
10. The ratio of 1,000 to $1/2$ is?

WEDNESDAY *Algebra*
Put on the board: x = 5   y = 8

1. $3x + 10y = ?$
2. $x^3 - 3y = ?$
3. $3x - 2y = ?$
4. $8x \div y = ?$
5. $5y \div x = ?$
6. $5x \times y = ?$
7. $x \div y = ?$
8. $x^3 - 10y = ?$
9. $10x \times 5y = ?$
10. $2x - 6.5 = ?$

THURSDAY *Integers*
Write True or False.

1. -3 plus (-8) = 11
2. +4 minus (-14) = 28
3. -60 divided by (-6) = 10
4. -15 times (+3) = 45
5. +15 times (-3) = 45
6. -10 squared = 100
7. 100 divided by (-25) = -4
8. -2 times (-3) times (-4) = 24
9. -180 divided by (-6) = 30
10. +200 plus (-200) = 400

FRIDAY *Patterns*
What's the next number?

1. 10, 20, 40, 80, 160, ___?
2. 6, 12, 24, 48, ___?
3. 1/3, 1, 1 1/3, 2, ___?
4. .3, .6, .9, ___?
5. 3, 7, 10, 13, 17, 20, __?
6. 707; 7,007; 70,007; 700,007; ___?
7. 100,000; 50,000; 25,000; ___?
8. 123, 234, 345, 456, ___?
9. 4, 15, 26, 37, 48, ___?
10. 0, 1, 1, 2, 3, 5, 8, 13, ___?

Fibonacci Numbers
0 + 1 = 1; 1 + 1= 2; 1 + 2 = 3; 2 + 3 = 5;
3 + 5 = 8; 5 + 8 = 13; 8 + 13 = 21

Answer Sheet: Name _____ Date _____

Mental Math Tip of the Week
Patterns In Math

$5 \times 4 = 20$	$30 \div 6 = 5$
$5 \times 40 = 200$	$300 \div 6 = 50$
$5 \times 400 = 2{,}000$	$3{,}000 \div 6 = 500$
$5 \times 4{,}000 = 20{,}000$	$30{,}000 \div 6 = 5{,}000$
$5 \times 40{,}000 = 200{,}000$	$300{,}000 \div 6 = 50{,}000$
$5 \times 400{,}000 = 2{,}000{,}000$	$3{,}000{,}000 \div 6 = 500{,}000$

Monday
1. _____
2. _____
3. _____
4. _____
5. _____
6. _____
7. _____
8. _____
9. _____
10. _____
Total correct _____

Tuesday
1. _____
2. _____
3. _____
4. _____
5. _____
6. _____
7. _____
8. _____
9. _____
10. _____
Total correct _____

Wednesday
1. _____
2. _____
3. _____
4. _____
5. _____
6. _____
7. _____
8. _____
9. _____
10. _____
Total correct _____

Thursday
1. _____
2. _____
3. _____
4. _____
5. _____
6. _____
7. _____
8. _____
9. _____
10. _____
Total correct _____

Friday
1. _____
2. _____
3. _____
4. _____
5. _____
6. _____
7. _____
8. _____
9. _____
10. _____
Total correct _____

Results–Correct Answers

Mon. _____

Tues. _____

Wed. _____

Thur. _____

Fri. _____

Total [ ]

Mental Math Tips of the Week

Adding Up & Subtracting

$2.99 + $2.99 is an easy mental math problem.
You simply add 1¢ to each of the $2.99's,
making the problem ($3.00 + $3.00 - 2¢),
making it ($6.00 - 2¢),
which is $5.98!

Making Problems Easy

All of you know how easy it is to multiply
4 x 25, so why should 12 x 25 be a problem?
Simply break down the problem to
(4 x 25) + (4 x 25) + (4 x 25),
which equals 100 + 100 + 100 = 300!

Monday

1. _____
2. _____
3. _____
4. _____
5. _____
6. _____
7. _____
8. _____
9. _____
10. _____

Total correct _____

Tuesday

1. _____
2. _____
3. _____
4. _____
5. _____
6. _____
7. _____
8. _____
9. _____
10. _____

Total correct _____

Wednesday

1. _____
2. _____
3. _____
4. _____
5. _____
6. _____
7. _____
8. _____
9. _____
10. _____

Total correct _____

Thursday

1. _____
2. _____
3. _____
4. _____
5. _____
6. _____
7. _____
8. _____
9. _____
10. _____

Total correct _____

Friday

1. _____
2. _____
3. _____
4. _____
5. _____
6. _____
7. _____
8. _____
9. _____
10. _____

Total correct _____

Results–Correct Answers

Mon. _____

Tues. _____

Wed. _____

Thur. _____

Fri. _____

Total

Answer Sheet: Name _____ Date _____

5 6 7,	3 0 9,	0 1 2,	8 4 8,	5	0	1
trillions	billions	millions	thousands	hundreds	tens	ones

1 .	3	6	7,	4	0	5
one	1/10	1/100	1/1,000	1/10,000	1/100,000	1/1,000,000

Monday

1. _____
2. _____
3. _____
4. _____
5. _____
6. _____
7. _____
8. _____
9. _____
10. _____

Total correct _____

Tuesday

1. _____
2. _____
3. _____
4. _____
5. _____
6. _____
7. _____
8. _____
9. _____
10. _____

Total correct _____

Wednesday

1. _____
2. _____
3. _____
4. _____
5. _____
6. _____
7. _____
8. _____
9. _____
10. _____

Total correct _____

Thursday

1. _____
2. _____
3. _____
4. _____
5. _____
6. _____
7. _____
8. _____
9. _____
10. _____

Total correct _____

Friday

1. _____
2. _____
3. _____
4. _____
5. _____
6. _____
7. _____
8. _____
9. _____
10. _____

Total correct _____

Results–Correct Answers

Mon. _____

Tues. _____

Wed. _____

Thur. _____

Fri. _____

Total [ ]

Mental Math Tips of the Week
Terminology

Addition	**Multiplication**
8 + 9 = 1 7	7 x 9 = 6 3
addend addend sum	factor factor product

Subtraction	**Division**
1 3 – 5 = 8	4 0 ÷ 5 = 8
minuend subtrahend difference	dividend divisor quotient

Monday
1. _____
2. _____
3. _____
4. _____
5. _____
6. _____
7. _____
8. _____
9. _____
10. _____

Total correct _____

Tuesday
1. _____
2. _____
3. _____
4. _____
5. _____
6. _____
7. _____
8. _____
9. _____
10. _____

Total correct _____

Wednesday
1. _____
2. _____
3. _____
4. _____
5. _____
6. _____
7. _____
8. _____
9. _____
10. _____

Total correct _____

Thursday
1. _____
2. _____
3. _____
4. _____
5. _____
6. _____
7. _____
8. _____
9. _____
10. _____

Total correct _____

Friday
1. _____
2. _____
3. _____
4. _____
5. _____
6. _____
7. _____
8. _____
9. _____
10. _____

Total correct _____

Results–Correct Answers

Mon. _____

Tues. _____

Wed. _____

Thur. _____

Fri. _____

Total

Mental Math Tip of the Week

Fraction = Decimal = Percent

1/2 = 0.5 = 50%	1/5 = 0.2 = 20%
1/4 = 0.25 = 25%	2/5 = 0.4 = 40%
3/4 = 0.75 = 75%	3/5 = 0.6 = 60%

Monday
1. _____
2. _____
3. _____
4. _____
5. _____
6. _____
7. _____
8. _____
9. _____
10. _____

Total correct _____

Tuesday
1. _____
2. _____
3. _____
4. _____
5. _____
6. _____
7. _____
8. _____
9. _____
10. _____

Total correct _____

Wednesday
1. _____
2. _____
3. _____
4. _____
5. _____
6. _____
7. _____
8. _____
9. _____
10. _____

Total correct _____

Thursday
1. _____
2. _____
3. _____
4. _____
5. _____
6. _____
7. _____
8. _____
9. _____
10. _____

Total correct _____

Friday
1. _____
2. _____
3. _____
4. _____
5. _____
6. _____
7. _____
8. _____
9. _____
10. _____

Total correct _____

Results–Correct Answers

Mon. _____

Tues. _____

Wed. _____

Thur. _____

Fri. _____

Total

Mental Math Tip of the Week

Temperature: Fahrenheit and Celsius

104°F = a very hot summer day = 40° C

87°F = a beautiful summer day = 30° C

68°F = a nice spring day = 20° C

50°F = a brisk autumn day = 10° C

32°F = freezing = 0° C

Monday

1. _____
2. _____
3. _____
4. _____
5. _____
6. _____
7. _____
8. _____
9. _____
10. _____

Total correct _____

Tuesday

1. _____
2. _____
3. _____
4. _____
5. _____
6. _____
7. _____
8. _____
9. _____
10. _____

Total correct _____

Wednesday

1. _____
2. _____
3. _____
4. _____
5. _____
6. _____
7. _____
8. _____
9. _____
10. _____

Total correct _____

Thursday

1. _____
2. _____
3. _____
4. _____
5. _____
6. _____
7. _____
8. _____
9. _____
10. _____

Total correct _____

Friday

1. _____
2. _____
3. _____
4. _____
5. _____
6. _____
7. _____
8. _____
9. _____
10. _____

Total correct _____

Results–Correct Answers

Mon. _____

Tues. _____

Wed. _____

Thur. _____

Fri. _____

Total

Mental Math Tips of the Week

Time

60 seconds = 1 minute	365 days = 1 year	**"30 days have September,**
60 minutes = 1 hour	366 days = 1 leap year	**April, June, & November.**
24 hours = 1 day	12 months = 1 year	**All the rest have 31,**
7 days = 1 week	10 years = 1 decade	**except February,**
13 weeks = 1 season	100 years = 1 century	**which has 28 . . .**
4 seasons = 1 year	10 centuries = 1 millennium	**and 29 on leap years."**

Monday
1. _____
2. _____
3. _____
4. _____
5. _____
6. _____
7. _____
8. _____
9. _____
10. _____

Total correct _____

Tuesday
1. _____
2. _____
3. _____
4. _____
5. _____
6. _____
7. _____
8. _____
9. _____
10. _____

Total correct _____

Wednesday
1. _____
2. _____
3. _____
4. _____
5. _____
6. _____
7. _____
8. _____
9. _____
10. _____

Total correct _____

Thursday
1. _____
2. _____
3. _____
4. _____
5. _____
6. _____
7. _____
8. _____
9. _____
10. _____

Total correct _____

Friday
1. _____
2. _____
3. _____
4. _____
5. _____
6. _____
7. _____
8. _____
9. _____
10. _____

Total correct _____

Results–Correct Answers

Mon. _____

Tues. _____

Wed. _____

Thur. _____

Fri. _____

Total

Answer Sheet: Name _____ Date _____

Mental Math Tip of the Week
3-Dimensional Figures

cone

cylinder

triangular prism

sphere

cube

triangular-based pyramid

square-based pyramid

rectangular prism

Monday
1. _____
2. _____
3. _____
4. _____
5. _____
6. _____
7. _____
8. _____
9. _____
10. _____

Total correct _____

Tuesday
1. _____
2. _____
3. _____
4. _____
5. _____
6. _____
7. _____
8. _____
9. _____
10. _____

Total correct _____

Wednesday
1. _____
2. _____
3. _____
4. _____
5. _____
6. _____
7. _____
8. _____
9. _____
10. _____

Total correct _____

Thursday
1. _____
2. _____
3. _____
4. _____
5. _____
6. _____
7. _____
8. _____
9. _____
10. _____

Total correct _____

Friday
1. _____
2. _____
3. _____
4. _____
5. _____
6. _____
7. _____
8. _____
9. _____
10. _____

Total correct _____

Results–Correct Answers

Mon. _____

Tues. _____

Wed. _____

Thur. _____

Fri. _____

Total

Answer Sheet: Name _____ Date _____

Mental Math Tip of the Week
Customary Measurement for Liquid Capacity

8 oz. = 1 cup   2 cups = 1 pint   2 pints = 1 quart   4 quarts = 1 gallon

Monday

1. _____
2. _____
3. _____
4. _____
5. _____
6. _____
7. _____
8. _____
9. _____
10. _____

Total correct _____

Tuesday

1. _____
2. _____
3. _____
4. _____
5. _____
6. _____
7. _____
8. _____
9. _____
10. _____

Total correct _____

Wednesday

1. _____
2. _____
3. _____
4. _____
5. _____
6. _____
7. _____
8. _____
9. _____
10. _____

Total correct _____

Thursday

1. _____
2. _____
3. _____
4. _____
5. _____
6. _____
7. _____
8. _____
9. _____
10. _____

Total correct _____

Friday

1. _____
2. _____
3. _____
4. _____
5. _____
6. _____
7. _____
8. _____
9. _____
10. _____

Total correct _____

Results–Correct Answers

Mon. _____

Tues. _____

Wed. _____

Thur. _____

Fri. _____

Total

Answer Sheet: Name _____ Date _____

Mental Math Tip of the Week
Metric and Customary Lengths

10 millimeters = 1 centimeter   2.5 centimeters = 1 inch   12 inches = 1 foot

100 centimeters = 1 meter   1 meter = 39 $\frac{1}{4}$ inches   3 feet (or 36 in.) = 1 yard

1,000 meters = 1 kilometer   1.6 kilometers = 1 mile   5,280 feet = 1 mile

.6 of a mile = 1 kilometer   10 soccer fields = 1 kilometer

Monday
1. _____
2. _____
3. _____
4. _____
5. _____
6. _____
7. _____
8. _____
9. _____
10. _____

Total correct _____

Tuesday
1. _____
2. _____
3. _____
4. _____
5. _____
6. _____
7. _____
8. _____
9. _____
10. _____

Total correct _____

Wednesday
1. _____
2. _____
3. _____
4. _____
5. _____
6. _____
7. _____
8. _____
9. _____
10. _____

Total correct _____

Thursday
1. _____
2. _____
3. _____
4. _____
5. _____
6. _____
7. _____
8. _____
9. _____
10. _____

Total correct _____

Friday
1. _____
2. _____
3. _____
4. _____
5. _____
6. _____
7. _____
8. _____
9. _____
10. _____

Total correct _____

Results–Correct Answers

Mon. _____

Tues. _____

Wed. _____

Thur. _____

Fri. _____

Total

70

Mental Math Tip of the Week
Types of Angles and Triangles

acute angle   right angle   obtuse angle   straight angle

right-angle triangle   isosceles triangle   equilateral triangle   scalene triangle

Monday
1. _____
2. _____
3. _____
4. _____
5. _____
6. _____
7. _____
8. _____
9. _____
10. _____

Total correct _____

Tuesday
1. _____
2. _____
3. _____
4. _____
5. _____
6. _____
7. _____
8. _____
9. _____
10. _____

Total correct _____

Wednesday
1. _____
2. _____
3. _____
4. _____
5. _____
6. _____
7. _____
8. _____
9. _____
10. _____

Total correct _____

Thursday
1. _____
2. _____
3. _____
4. _____
5. _____
6. _____
7. _____
8. _____
9. _____
10. _____

Total correct _____

Friday
1. _____
2. _____
3. _____
4. _____
5. _____
6. _____
7. _____
8. _____
9. _____
10. _____

Total correct _____

Results–Correct Answers

Mon. _____

Tues. _____

Wed. _____

Thur. _____

Fri. _____

Total

Mental Math Tip of the Week

Quadrilaterals

rectangle   rhombus   square   parallelogram   trapezoid

Monday	Tuesday	Wednesday
1. _____	1. _____	1. _____
2. _____	2. _____	2. _____
3. _____	3. _____	3. _____
4. _____	4. _____	4. _____
5. _____	5. _____	5. _____
6. _____	6. _____	6. _____
7. _____	7. _____	7. _____
8. _____	8. _____	8. _____
9. _____	9. _____	9. _____
10. _____	10. _____	10. _____
Total correct _____	Total correct _____	Total correct _____

Thursday	Friday	Results–Correct Answers
1. _____	1. _____	Mon. _____
2. _____	2. _____	
3. _____	3. _____	Tues. _____
4. _____	4. _____	
5. _____	5. _____	Wed. _____
6. _____	6. _____	
7. _____	7. _____	Thur. _____
8. _____	8. _____	
9. _____	9. _____	Fri. _____
10. _____	10. _____	
Total correct _____	Total correct _____	*Total* [ ]

Mental Math Tip of the Week
Polygons

triangle

pentagon

quadrilateral

hexagon

octagon

heptagon

nonagon

dodecagon

decagon

Monday

1. _____
2. _____
3. _____
4. _____
5. _____
6. _____
7. _____
8. _____
9. _____
10. _____

Total correct _____

Tuesday

1. _____
2. _____
3. _____
4. _____
5. _____
6. _____
7. _____
8. _____
9. _____
10. _____

Total correct _____

Wednesday

1. _____
2. _____
3. _____
4. _____
5. _____
6. _____
7. _____
8. _____
9. _____
10. _____

Total correct _____

Thursday

1. _____
2. _____
3. _____
4. _____
5. _____
6. _____
7. _____
8. _____
9. _____
10. _____

Total correct _____

Friday

1. _____
2. _____
3. _____
4. _____
5. _____
6. _____
7. _____
8. _____
9. _____
10. _____

Total correct _____

Results–Correct Answers

Mon. _____

Tues. _____

Wed. _____

Thur. _____

Fri. _____

Total

Answer Sheet: Name _____ Date _____

Mental Math Tip of the Week
The Circle

circumference—the perimeter around a circle

semicircle—half of a circle

diameter—the distance across a circle through its center

radius—the distance from the center of a circle to its circumference

arc—a portion of a circle along its circumference

quadrant—1 of 4 equal regions of a circle

Monday
1. _____
2. _____
3. _____
4. _____
5. _____
6. _____
7. _____
8. _____
9. _____
10. _____

Total correct _____

Tuesday
1. _____
2. _____
3. _____
4. _____
5. _____
6. _____
7. _____
8. _____
9. _____
10. _____

Total correct _____

Wednesday
1. _____
2. _____
3. _____
4. _____
5. _____
6. _____
7. _____
8. _____
9. _____
10. _____

Total correct _____

Thursday
1. _____
2. _____
3. _____
4. _____
5. _____
6. _____
7. _____
8. _____
9. _____
10. _____

Total correct _____

Friday
1. _____
2. _____
3. _____
4. _____
5. _____
6. _____
7. _____
8. _____
9. _____
10. _____

Total correct _____

Results–Correct Answers

Mon. _____

Tues. _____

Wed. _____

Thur. _____

Fri. _____

Total

Mental Math Tip of the Week
Plane Geometry Formulas

To find the perimeter of a square, multiply the length of a side by 4.

To find the perimeter of a triangle, add the length of the 3 sides.

l

d

l

l

w

To find the circumference of a circle, multiply the diameter by pi (3.14).

To find the perimeter of a rectangle, use the formula $2(l) + 2(w) =$ perimeter.

Monday	**Tuesday**	**Wednesday**
1. _____	1. _____	1. _____
2. _____	2. _____	2. _____
3. _____	3. _____	3. _____
4. _____	4. _____	4. _____
5. _____	5. _____	5. _____
6. _____	6. _____	6. _____
7. _____	7. _____	7. _____
8. _____	8. _____	8. _____
9. _____	9. _____	9. _____
10. _____	10. _____	10. _____
Total correct _____	Total correct _____	Total correct _____

Thursday	**Friday**	*Results–Correct Answers*
1. _____	1. _____	Mon. _____
2. _____	2. _____	
3. _____	3. _____	Tues. _____
4. _____	4. _____	
5. _____	5. _____	Wed. _____
6. _____	6. _____	
7. _____	7. _____	Thur. _____
8. _____	8. _____	
9. _____	9. _____	Fri. _____
10. _____	10. _____	
Total correct _____	Total correct _____	*Total*

WEEK 1

MONDAY
1. 91
2. 901
3. 910
4. 9,001
5. 9,010
6. 53
7. 503
8. 530
9. 5,003
10. 50,303

TUESDAY
1. 555
2. 656
3. 198
4. 847
5. 909
6. 1,403
7. 2,790
8. 6,066
9. 10,234
10. 12,345

WEDNESDAY
1. 3
2. 100
3. 10
4. 4
5. 4
6. 0
7. 7
8. 12
9. 12
10. 3

THURSDAY
1. 24
2. 365
3. 2
4. 6
5. 5
6. 10
7. 5
8. 100
9. 50
10. 4

FRIDAY
1. 37
2. 44
3. 19
4. 24
5. 31
6. 42
7. 50
8. 60
9. 100
10. 109

WEEK 2

MONDAY
1. 0
2. 6
3. 12
4. 20
5. 40
6. 80
7. 100
8. 120
9. 200
10. 400

TUESDAY
1. 6
2. 60
3. 600
4. 100
5. 1,000
6. 10,000
7. 18
8. 180
9. 1,800
10. 18,000

WEDNESDAY
1. 70 ¢
2. 80 ¢
3. 30 ¢
4. 10 ¢
5. 60 ¢
6. 40 ¢
7. $1.00
8. 10 ¢
9. 20 ¢
10. 25 ¢

THURSDAY
1. 5
2. 10
3. 50
4. 500
5. 10
6. 100
7. 1,000
8. 100
9. 1,000
10. 10,000

FRIDAY
1. 3
2. 4
3. 0
4. 7
5. 3
6. 9
7. 30
8. 20
9. 0
10. 14

WEEK 3

MONDAY
1. 803
2. 8,003
3. 80,003
4. 80,303
5. 800,300
6. 684
7. 973
8. 7,605
9. 43,210
10. 500,505

TUESDAY
1. 40
2. 60
3. 400
4. 900
5. 4,000
6. 50
7. 100
8. 150
9. 9,000
10. 9,999

WEDNESDAY
1. 3 dimes
2. 2 quarters
3. dime & 2 pennies
4. 2 nickels & 2 pennies
5. 2 dimes & 1 nickel
6. 5 nickels
7. 2 dimes & 5 pennies
8. 1 dm., 2 nick. & 5 pen.
9. 4 nickels & 5 pennies
10. 10 pen. & 3 nick.

THURSDAY
1. 80 cents
2. $1.50
3. $3.00
4. $1.50
5. $2.00
6. $2.00
7. $10.00
8. $3.60
9. $4.50
10. $18.00

FRIDAY
1. Tues.
2. March
3. Earth
4. Friday
5. May
6. Mars
7. Feb.
8. 60
9. 60
10. 24

WEEK 4

MONDAY
1. 4
2. 2
3. 6
4. 4
5. 3
6. 2
7. 2
8. 3
9. 5
10. 10

TUESDAY
1. 10
2. 16
3. 25
4. 21
5. 20
6. 18
7. 40
8. 55
9. 40
10. 61

WEDNESDAY
1. 8
2. 20
3. 12
4. 4
5. 14
6. 20
7. 600
8. 800
9. 1,000
10. 2,000

THURSDAY
1. 2
2. 3
3. 6
4. 3
5. 6
6. 20
7. 200
8. 3,000
9. 40,000
10. 2 million

FRIDAY
1. 9
2. 50
3. 12
4. 3
5. 36
6. 100
7. 1,000
8. 2,000
9. 365
10. 30

WEEK 5

MONDAY
1. 30
2. 30
3. 40
4. 40
5. 60
6. 60
7. 800
8. 800
9. 10,000
10. 10,000

TUESDAY
1. 9
2. 900
3. 16
4. 1,600
5. 25
6. 2,500
7. 4,000
8. 9,000
9. 16,000
10. 25,000

WEDNESDAY
1. 21
2. 7
3. 35
4. 5
5. 40
6. 150
7. 40
8. 4
9. 25
10. 600

THURSDAY
1. 183
2. 359
3. 202
4. 1,486
5. 9,050
6. 509
7. 158,630
8. 36,201
9. 2,543,460
10. 9,009,009

FRIDAY
1. 1
2. 2
3. 3
4. 3
5. 3
6. 4
7. 27
8. 10
9. 7
10. 1

WEEK 6

MONDAY
1. 15
2. 24
3. 36
4. 21
5. 24
6. 20
7. 28
8. 25
9. 16
10. 27

TUESDAY
1. 10
2. 10
3. 10
4. 20
5. 5
6. 10
7. 20
8. 10
9. 15
10. 25

WEDNESDAY
1. 3 x 10
2. 5 x 4
3. 5 x 5
4. 4 x 4
5. 2 x 11
6. 5 x 5
7. 2 x 12
8. 7 x 5
9. 7 x 7
10. 9 x 2

THURSDAY
1. 3
2. 4
3. 0
4. 4
5. 5
6. 6
7. 8
8. 0
9. 4
10. 7

FRIDAY
1. 30
2. 6
3. 50
4. 6
5. 50
6. 10
7. 5
8. 6
9. 50
10. 3 1/2

WEEK 7

MONDAY
1. 30
2. 40
3. 10
4. 0
5. 100
6. 200
7. 400
8. 2
9. 1
10. 20

TUESDAY
1. 40
2. 50
3. 10
4. 90
5. 60
6. 60
7. 20
8. 0
9. 80
10. 100

WEDNESDAY
1. 12
2. 12
3. 21
4. 70
5. 365
6. 366
7. 2
8. 3
9. 4
10. 8

THURSDAY
1. 16
2. 2
3. 40
4. 10
5. 48
6. 20
7. 500
8. 200
9. 9,000
10. 2,000

FRIDAY
1. 7
2. 28
3. 15
4. 60
5. 100
6. 400
7. 2,000
8. 8,000
9. 25,000
10. 1,000,000

WEEK 8

MONDAY
1. 10
2. 20
3. 24
4. 30
5. 100
6. 60
7. 150
8. 600
9. 100
10. 400

TUESDAY
1. 36, 58, 60
2. 99, 101, 103
3. 36, 47, 48
4. 70, 78, 91
5. 18, 22, 27
6. 178, 180, 184
7. 158, 161, 166
8. 355, 535, 553
9. 404, 440, 444
10. 890, 980, 998

WEDNESDAY
1. =
2. not
3. not
4. =
5. =
6. =
7. =
8. not
9. not
10. =

THURSDAY
1. 1
2. 2
3. 14
4. 17
5. 1
6. 5
7. 4
8. 31
9. 4th
10. 31

FRIDAY
1. 20
2. 30
3. 10"
4. 30"
5. 75¢
6. $3.00
7. 50 cm
8. 9 mos.
9. 8 yrs.
10. 99 yrs.

WEEK 9

MONDAY
1. 8
2. 27
3. 1
4. 24
5. 40
6. 60
7. 90
8. 250
9. 500
10. 1,000

TUESDAY
1. 15
2. 20
3. 15
4. 24
5. 80
6. 9
7. 900
8. 200
9. 1,000
10. 16

WEDNESDAY
1. kg.
2. liter
3. inch
4. 5 x 5
5. 5 nickels
6. 5 x 10
7. mile
8. 8 dimes
9. Jan.
10. meter

THURSDAY
1. quarters
2. cm.
3. meters
4. feet
5. pennies
6. days
7. months
8. hours
9. minute
10. Feb.

FRIDAY
1. 1
2. 4
3. 9
4. 16
5. 25
6. 36
7. 100
8. 20
9. 125
10. 5 x 5

WEEK 10

MONDAY
1. 14
2. 50
3. 25
4. 3
5. 6
6. 4
7. 5 cents
8. 250 cents
9. pint
10. 12

TUESDAY
1. 2
2. 3
3. 4
4. 5
5. 6
6. 7
7. 8
8. 9
9. 10
10. 12

WEDNESDAY
1. 3
2. 2
3. 15
4. 5
5. 6
6. 3
7. 8
8. 6
9. 10
10. 5

THURSDAY
1. F
2. T
3. F
4. F
5. F
6. F
7. F
8. T
9. F
10. F

FRIDAY
1. 20
2. 24
3. 24
4. 28
5. 22
6. 20
7. 0
8. 24
9. 808
10. 128

WEEK 11

MONDAY
1. 4
2. 5
3. 6
4. 3
5. 12
6. 12
7. 10
8. 10
9. 12
10. 25

TUESDAY
1. 10
2. 10
3. 5
4. 4
5. 10
6. 40
7. 10
8. 22
9. 50
10. 100

WEDNESDAY
1. 25
2. 5
3. 9
4. 13
5. 50
6. 3
7. 7
8. 52
9. 365
10. 4

THURSDAY
1. 1/7
2. 1/2
3. 1/4
4. 1/10
5. 1/12
6. 1/4
7. 1/100
8. 1/5
9. 1/10
10. 1/12

FRIDAY
1. 25
2. 50
3. 100
4. 250
5. 500
6. 1,000
7. 5,000
8. 50,000
9. 500,000
10. 5,000,000

WEEK 12

MONDAY
1. 20
2. 30
3. 40
4. 17
5. 21
6. 70
7. 300
8. 800
9. 4,000
10. 2,000,000

TUESDAY
1. 40
2. 1
3. 22
4. 16
5. 30
6. 75
7. 50
8. 800
9. 3,000
10. 700,000

WEDNESDAY
1. 10
2. 20
3. 12
4. 3
5. 5,280
6. 100
7. 1,000
8. 60
9. 60
10. 24

THURSDAY
1. 1/4
2. 1/2
3. 1/2
4. 1/10
5. 1/10
6. 1/5
7. 1/100
8. 6/12 or 1/2
9. 2/4 or 1/2
10. 10/20 or 1/2

FRIDAY
1. 150
2. 200
3. 1,500
4. 2,000
5. 15,000
6. 20,000
7. 150,000
8. 200,000
9. 1,500,000
10. 2,000,000

WEEK 13

MONDAY
1. 4
2. 3
3. 0
4. 4
5. 8
6. 7
7. 31
8. 30
9. 365
10. 366

TUESDAY
1. 9
2. 16
3. 25
4. 36
5. 49
6. 64
7. 81
8. 100
9. 400
10. 900

WEDNESDAY
1. 9
2. 3
3. 18
4. 2
5. 12
6. 4
7. 32
8. 2
9. 900
10. 50

THURSDAY
1. II
2. III
3. IV
4. V
5. VI
6. VIII
7. IX
8. X
9. XII
10. XV

FRIDAY
1. $1.50
2. $6.00
3. $10.50
4. $7.50
5. 50¢
6. $4.00
7. $11.00
8. $8.00
9. $2.00
10. $15.00

WEEK 14

MONDAY
1. T
2. T
3. F
4. T
5. F
6. T
7. F
8. F
9. T
10. F

TUESDAY
1. no
2. yes
3. yes
4. yes
5. yes
6. yes
7. no
8. no
9. yes
10. yes

WEDNESDAY
1. inch
2. meter
3. meter
4. mile
5. ounce
6. kg.
7. liter
8. gallon
9. metric tonne
10. 100 meter

THURSDAY
1. 50¢
2. 5¢
3. 0
4. 30¢
5. 70¢
6. 95¢
7. 40¢
8. 70¢
9. $1.00
10. 15¢

FRIDAY
1. $8.00
2. 50¢
3. $13.00
4. $1.50
5. $5.50
6. $12.00
7. $4.00
8. $10.00
9. $5.00
10. 0

WEEK 15

MONDAY
1. 3,002
2. 5,602
3. 45,089
4. 97,130
5. 205,671
6. 891,043
7. 1,650,730
8. 3,078,654
9. 62,400,002
10. 123,456,789

TUESDAY
1. 60
2. 90
3. 120
4. 150
5. 360
6. 450
7. 140
8. 200
9. 250
10. 100

WEDNESDAY
1. 1
2. 4
3. 9
4. 16
5. 25
6. 36
7. 49
8. 64
9. 81
10. 100

THURSDAY
1. circle
2. oval
3. square
4. pentagon
5. hexagon
6. heptagon
7. octagon
8. 2 parallel lines
9. 2 intersecting lines
10. right angle

FRIDAY
1. 30
2. 30
3. 12
4. 14
5. 6
6. 5
7. 5
8. 5
9. $500,000
10. $500,000,000

WEEK 16

MONDAY
1. 42
2. 36
3. 30
4. 56
5. 56
6. 63
7. 48
8. 54
9. 32
10. 72

TUESDAY
1. 5
2. 7
3. 8
4. 9
5. 9
6. 9
7. 5
8. 7
9. 5
10. 7

WEDNESDAY
1. 55
2. 85
3. 100
4. 150
5. 175
6. 300
7. 580
8. 1,000
9. 11,400
10. 55,000

THURSDAY
1. 3
2. 2
3. 6
4. 4
5. 5
6. 5
7. 6
8. 3
9. 1
10. 3

FRIDAY
1. 200
2. 48
3. 9
4. 600
5. 12
6. 24
7. 400
8. 3,000
9. 10,000
10. 72

WEEK 17

MONDAY
1. 300
2. 3,000
3. 30,000
4. 240
5. 2,400
6. 24,000
7. 360
8. 3,600
9. 36,000
10. 3,600

TUESDAY
1. 5
2. 50
3. 500
4. 5
5. 50
6. 5,000
7. 5,000,000
8. 10
9. 100
10. 10,000

WEDNESDAY
1. 35
2. 44
3. 20
4. 85
5. 40
6. 25
7. 1,400
8. 1,500
9. 7,400
10. 700,000

THURSDAY
1. 9
2. 7
3. 36
4. 15
5. 4
6. 2
7. 7
8. 35
9. 20
10. 48

FRIDAY
1. $1.50
2. $3.50
3. $16.00
4. $61.00
5. $17.00
6. $21.75
7. $2.00
8. $2.50
9. $12.12
10. $15.15

WEEK 18

MONDAY
1. 1,800
2. 18,000
3. 200
4. 2,000
5. 10,000
6. 100,000
7. 40
8. 400
9. 4,000
10. 40,000

TUESDAY
1. 8
2. 13
3. 25
4. 29
5. 9
6. 40
7. 50
8. 40
9. 99
10. 125

WEDNESDAY
1. 105
2. 305
3. 666
4. 608
5. 10,500
6. 24,000
7. 900
8. 300
9. 999
10. 850,000

THURSDAY
1. 2
2. 4
3. 20
4. 12
5. 50
6. 7
7. 4
8. 3
9. 5
10. 8

FRIDAY
1. $9.00
2. $22.00
3. $30.00
4. $19.00
5. $97.00
6. $300.00
7. $200.00
8. $50.00
9. $350.00
10. 1¢

WEEK 19

MONDAY
1. T
2. T
3. F
4. T
5. F
6. T
7. T
8. T
9. F
10. T

TUESDAY
1. 40
2. 444
3. 404
4. 4,004
5. 44,444
6. 2,222
7. 2,002,002
8. 2,022
9. 66
10. 666

WEDNESDAY
1. 149
2. 80
3. 60
4. 50
5. 100
6. 4
7. 25
8. 25
9. 90
10. 50

THURSDAY
1. $2.40
2. $2.50
3. $1.98
4. $7.98
5. $3.96
6. $3.00
7. $6.10
8. $7.00
9. $4.95
10. $2.80

FRIDAY
1. 150
2. 370
3. 990
4. 1,500
5. 1,900
6. 1,990
7. 1,999
8. 5,000
9. 2,500
10. 2,000,000

WEEK 20

MONDAY
1. 1/2
2. 3/4
3. 1/4
4. 4/5
5. 7/8
6. 9/10
7. 1/10
8. 1/5
9. 1/8
10. 1 1/2

TUESDAY
1. 60
2. 600
3. 6,000
4. 200
5. 2,000
6. 2,000,000
7. 300
8. 30,000
9. 3,000,000
10. 30,000,000

WEDNESDAY
1. 5
2. 21
3. 10
4. 20
5. 15
6. 10
7. 5
8. 0
9. 40
10. 350

THURSDAY
1. 2
2. 5
3. 5
4. 5
5. 2
6. 4
7. 4
8. 4
9. 2
10. $13.00 each

FRIDAY
1. 3
2. 1/12
3. 30
4. 15
5. 20
6. 1/12
7. 1/3
8. 1/100
9. 1/4
10. 9:30 a.m.

WEEK 21

MONDAY
1. 9
2. 18
3. 20
4. 100
5. 30
6. 20
7. 25
8. 15
9. 18
10. 20

TUESDAY
1. no
2. yes
3. no
4. yes
5. yes
6. yes
7. yes
8. no
9. yes
10. yes

WEDNESDAY
1. 20¢
2. 95¢
3. $1.05
4. $2.00
5. $1.00
6. $2.75
7. 20¢
8. $1.00
9. 50¢
10. $1.60

THURSDAY
1. 40 m
2. 1 h 15 m
3. 1 h 45 m
4. 2 h 30 m
5. 3 h 30 m
6. 4 h 30 m
7. 7 h
8. 3 h 15 m
9. 12 h
10. 12 h

FRIDAY
1. 6
2. 4
3. 15
4. 100
5. 1/2
6. 5
7. 50
8. quarter
9. dime
10. 500,000

WEEK 22

MONDAY
1. 40
2. 75
3. 19
4. 150
5. 40
6. 40
7. 65
8. 50
9. 20
10. 100

TUESDAY
1. yes
2. no
3. yes
4. no
5. no
6. yes
7. yes
8. yes
9. yes
10. yes

WEDNESDAY
1. $3.75
2. $8.75
3. $11.40
4. $14.25
5. $21.50
6. $4.60
7. $49.50
8. $73.00
9. $90.00
10. $68.00

THURSDAY
1. 5 h
2. 6 h
3. 3 h 30 m
4. 6 h
5. 2 h 30 m
6. 5 h 30 m
7. 5 h 30 m
8. 7 h 45 m
9. 8 h
10. 1 m

FRIDAY
1. 50 yrs.
2. 2 yrs.
3. 50¢
4. 20¢
5. $2.50
6. $1.00
7. $10.00
8. $4.00
9. $50.00
10. $20.00

WEEK 23

MONDAY
1. 4
2. 90
3. 20
4. 25
5. 50
6. 70
7. 200
8. 500
9. 300
10. 70,000

TUESDAY
1. 210
2. 2,100
3. 21,000
4. 21,000,000
5. 480
6. 4,800
7. 48,000
8. 48,000,000
9. 8,100,000
10. 81,000,000

WEDNESDAY
1. .20
2. .10
3. .30
4. .50
5. .40
6. .60
7. .75
8. .80
9. .90
10. .99

THURSDAY
1. 100
2. 30
3. 150
4. 6
5. 16
6. 5
7. 50
8. 10
9. 16 in.
10. 15 sq. in.

FRIDAY
1. 24
2. 365
3. 366
4. 52
5. 12
6. 7
7. 4
8. 10
9. 100
10. 1,000

WEEK 24

MONDAY
1. 4
2. 90
3. 900
4. 45
5. 25
6. 30
7. 600
8. 4,500
9. 500
10. 15,000

TUESDAY
1. 3
2. 30
3. 300
4. 7
5. 70
6. 700
7. 9
8. 90
9. 9,000
10. 9,000,000

WEDNESDAY
1. 12
2. 6
3. 6
4. 26
5. 14
6. 15
7. 2
8. 5
9. 50
10. 500

THURSDAY
1. 63
2. 5
3. 17
4. 97
5. 36
6. 9
7. 500
8. 74
9. 20 in.
10. 21 sq. in.

FRIDAY
1. 120
2. 800
3. 599
4. 115
5. 765
6. 699
7. 1,099
8. 1,300
9. 19,000
10. 170,000

WEEK 25

MONDAY
1. 8
2. 5
3. 4
4. 9
5. 8
6. 7
7. 10
8. 2
9. 3
10. 4

TUESDAY
1. 1,000 lbs.
2. 50 cm.
3. 50 yrs.
4. 25 yrs.
5. 75 yrs.
6. 750 grams
7. 500 m.
8. 250 m.
9. 1 mm.
10. 90 cm.

WEDNESDAY
1. 10
2. 200
3. 300
4. 750
5. 1/2 or 2/4
6. 3/8
7. Weds.
8. 1950
9. 70 degrees
10. April 15

THURSDAY
1. $1.98
2. $5.98
3. $3.96
4. $1.47
5. $4.95
6. $1.96
7. $4.90
8. $29.97
9. $49.98
10. $599.98

FRIDAY
1. 2 h 30 m
2. 11 h
3. 48 h
4. 240 h
5. 4
6. 2 yrs.
7. 120 mos.
8. This year minus 11.
9. This year minus 100.
10. This year plus 10.

WEEK 26

MONDAY
1. 10
2. 6
3. 3
4. 40
5. 8
6. 80
7. 4
8. 1,000
9. 10,000
10. 1,000,000

TUESDAY
1. $1.45
2. 85¢
3. 25¢
4. $1.25
5. $1.80
6. $20.00
7. $320.00
8. $84.00
9. $76.00
10. 160

WEDNESDAY
1. 300,000
2. $350.00
3. 1/2
4. 3/5
5. Wed.
6. May
7. 8 p.m.
8. 6 feet
9. 1600
10. 500,000

THURSDAY
1. 24
2. 13
3. 99
4. 25
5. 125
6. 4
7. 6
8. 10
9. 9
10. 8

FRIDAY
1. 200
2. 300
3. 2,000
4. 20,000
5. 200,000
6. 2,000,000
7. 20,000,000
8. $20,000
9. $180,000
10. $600,000

WEEK 27

MONDAY
1. 6
2. 60
3. 61
4. 63
5. 7
6. 70
7. 71
8. 9
9. 90
10. 91

TUESDAY
1. .20
2. .10
3. .30
4. .50
5. .40
6. .60
7. .75
8. .80
9. .90
10. .99

WEDNESDAY
1. 20 %
2. 10 %
3. 30 %
4. 50 %
5. 40 %
6. 60 %
7. 75 %
8. 80 %
9. 90 %
10. 99 %

THURSDAY
1. 20
2. 25
3. 125
4. 1,250
5. 5
6. 50
7. 245
8. 2,495
9. 50,000
10. 1,250,000

FRIDAY
1. $3.00
2. $1.90
3. $9.00
4. $4.50
5. $3.00
6. $30.00
7. $45.00
8. $3.60
9. $1.60
10. $6.00

WEEK 28

MONDAY
1. 200
2. 2,000
3. 2,000
4. 20,000
5. 200,000
6. 2,000,000
7. 8
8. 8
9. 8
10. 8,000

TUESDAY
1. 27
2. 160
3. 60
4. 120
5. 64
6. 150
7. 250
8. 1,000
9. 25,000
10. 1,000,000

WEDNESDAY
1. 60
2. 240
3. 60
4. 30
5. 600
6. 24
7. 12
8. 240
9. 21
10. 77

THURSDAY
1. L
2. C
3. XV
4. D
5. MMD
6. V
7. II
8. C
9. V
10. DC

FRIDAY
1. 26
2. 51
3. 6
4. 32
5. 60
6. 90
7. 125
8. 2
9. 100
10. 5

WEEK 29

MONDAY
1. not
2. not
3. not
4. not
5. not
6. not
7. =
8. =
9. not
10. not

TUESDAY
1. 19
2. 8
3. 24
4. 30
5. 50
6. 4
7. 35
8. 48
9. 38
10. 0

WEDNESDAY
1. XI
2. XXI
3. VI
4. C
5. DC
6. LX
7. XXVIII
8. LXXXV
9. X
10. MCXI

THURSDAY
1. L
2. X
3. XXX
4. DCC
5. L
6. LXX
7. M
8. II
9. M
10. MMM

FRIDAY
1. 1,500
2. 750
3. 4,000
4. 10,000
5. 50,050
6. 99,999
7. 1,000,000
8. 10,000,000
9. 10,000,010
10. 9,999,999

WEEK 30

MONDAY
1. 225
2. 306
3. 312
4. 357
5. 385
6. 280
7. 198
8. 189
9. 198
10. 396

TUESDAY
1. 2
2. 4
3. 4
4. 4
5. 3
6. 5
7. 2
8. 7
9. 6
10. 10

WEDNESDAY
1. $3.50
2. $5.01
3. $10.01
4. $15.00
5. $1.50
6. $1.02
7. $1.25
8. $2.50
9. 1¢
10. $31.00

THURSDAY
1. 6
2. 24
3. 18
4. 36
5. 72
6. 12
7. 24
8. 18
9. 72
10. 3

FRIDAY
1. $1.01
2. $1.51
3. no
4. yes
5. 8
6. 77
7. 400
8. 37
9. 13
10. 2,000

WEEK 31

MONDAY
1. 350
2. 200
3. 30
4. 11,000
5. 500,000
6. 450,000
7. 300
8. 200
9. 125
10. 3,000

TUESDAY
1. 1/4
2. 1/2
3. 1 or 4/4
4. 3/4
5. 2 1/2 or 2 2/4
6. 1/4
7. 6/10
8. 6/10
9. 9/10
10. 4/10

WEDNESDAY
1. 9
2. 90
3. 60
4. 600
5. 36
6. 10
7. 36
8. 36
9. 360,000
10. 6,000,000

THURSDAY
1. 7
2. 1
3. 10, 11, 12
4. 3/4
5. 81
6. 0
7. 0
8. inch
9. meter
10. quart

FRIDAY
1. 92
2. 5 x 11
3. 360
4. 1/3 of 900
5. 8 x 50
6. 28.1
7. 1 gal.
8. 2 km
9. 3 tons
10. 2 $20 bills

WEEK 32

MONDAY
1. 70,707
2. 100's
3. LXVII
4. 2/5
5. 25 %
6. 1/4 or 25/100
7. 99, 98, 97
8. 1/10
9. 246
10. 3/4

TUESDAY
1. F
2. T
3. T
4. T
5. F
6. F
7. T
8. T
9. F
10. T

WEDNESDAY
1. T
2. F
3. T
4. T
5. F
6. F
7. F
8. T
9. F
10. T

THURSDAY
1. 8 x 7
2. 3 x 12
3. 62
4. 92
5. 32
6. 5 dozen
7. 4 dimes & 11 cents
8. XVI
9. 150 min.
10. millennium

FRIDAY
1. 8
2. 31
3. 90
4. 360
5. 3
6. 8
7. 365
8. 52
9. 6
10. 2

WEEK 33

MONDAY
1. yes
2. no
3. yes
4. no
5. no
6. no
7. yes
8. no
9. yes
10. no

TUESDAY
1. 6
2. 12
3. 34
4. 20
5. 120
6. 60
7. 40
8. 6,000
9. 10
10. 6

WEDNESDAY
1. 1,500
2. 150
3. 18
4. 54
5. 6
6. 1,500
7. 90
8. 90
9. 150
10. 150

THURSDAY
1. 8 x 8
2. 3 x 120
3. 42
4. 82
5. 52
6. 72
7. 3 quarters
8. October
9. 3 hrs.
10. 15 centuries

FRIDAY
1. rectangle
2. pentagon
3. right angle
4. semcircle
5. triangle
6. octagon
7. oval
8. 2 parallel lines
9. hexagon
10. 2 intersecting lines

WEEK 34

MONDAY
1. 17
2. 170
3. 1,700
4. 72
5. 7,200
6. 720,000
7. 1,000
8. 8,200
9. 8,920
10. 8,999,992

TUESDAY
1. no
2. no
3. yes
4. no
5. yes
6. no
7. no
8. no
9. yes
10. no

WEDNESDAY
1. $5.00
2. $12.00
3. $2.18
4. $2.97
5. $5.50
6. $6.00
7. $90.00
8. $98.00
9. $398.00
10. $30,000

THURSDAY
1. 50 %
2. 25 %
3. 20 %
4. 10 %
5. 20 %
6. 30 %
7. 40 %
8. 50 %
9. 70 %
10. 90 %

FRIDAY
1. right angle
2. circle
3. triangle
4. radius
5. parallel
6. 8
7. sphere
8. oval
9. cube
10. cone

WEEK 35

MONDAY
1. yes
2. yes
3. no
4. yes
5. no
6. yes
7. no
8. no
9. no
10. no

TUESDAY
1. $50
2. $25
3. $10
4. $25
5. $2
6. $10
7. $15
8. $1
9. $20
10. $100

WEDNESDAY
1. T
2. T
3. F
4. F
5. F
6. F
7. F
8. T
9. T
10. F

THURSDAY
1. F
2. T
3. F
4. F
5. F
6. T
7. T
8. T
9. F
10. T

FRIDAY
1. right angle
2. square
3. parallel
4. radius
5. yard
6. year
7. ton
8. quart
9. century
10. Thanksgiving

WEEK 36

MONDAY
1. 1/4
2. 10
3. 1 1/2
4. 12
5. 20
6. 3
7. 1/4
8. 1 1/4 or 5/4
9. 1 1/4 or 5/4
10. 6 m

TUESDAY
1. $5.50
2. $2.50
3. $100.00
4. 50¢
5. $30.00
6. $2.50
7. $250.00
8. $11.00
9. $33.00
10. $90.00

WEDNESDAY
1. T
2. F
3. T
4. F
5. T
6. F
7. F
8. F
9. F
10. T

THURSDAY
1. F
2. T
3. T
4. T
5. T
6. T
7. T
8. T
9. T
10. T

FRIDAY
1. obtuse
2. equilateral triangle
3. intersecting lines
4. diameter
5. 1 mile
6. leap year
7. metric tonne
8. gallon
9. decade
10. Jan. 1st

WEEK 37

MONDAY
1. 8
2. 27
3. 125
4. 1,000
5. 900
6. 100
7. 12
8. 3^2
9. 10^2
10. 1,000,000

TUESDAY
1. 1 1/2
2. 25
3. 60
4. 1,200
5. 15,000
6. 70,000
7. 1,200,000
8. 25,000,000
9. 400,000,000
10. 500,000,000

WEDNESDAY
1. 8
2. 3
3. 5
4. 4
5. 2
6. 2
7. 5,280
8. 52
9. 20
10. 500

THURSDAY
1. yes
2. yes
3. no
4. yes
5. no
6. yes
7. yes
8. no
9. no
10. yes

FRIDAY
1. T
2. T
3. F
4. T
5. T
6. F
7. T
8. F
9. F
10. T

WEEK 38

MONDAY
1. 1
2. 24
3. 120
4. 1,000
5. 1,110
6. 150
7. 16
8. 3^3
9. 120
10. 1,000,000

TUESDAY
1. 10
2. 30
3. 40
4. 111
5. 120
6. 2,000
7. 30,000
8. 111,111
9. 333,333,333
10. 1 trillion

WEDNESDAY
1. 3
2. 4
3. 2
4. 4
5. 10
6. 10
7. 24
8. 31
9. 13
10. 3,600

THURSDAY
1. $2.49
2. $3.25
3. $2.75
4. 80¢
5. $1.20
6. $3.80
7. $4.45
8. $22.50
9. $13.01
10. $6.90

FRIDAY
1. F
2. F
3. T
4. F
5. T
6. T
7. F
8. T
9. T
10. T

WEEK 39

MONDAY
1. T
2. T
3. F
4. F
5. T
6. F
7. T
8. T
9. F
10. F

TUESDAY
1. 2 1/2
2. 2 1/3
3. 2 1/4
4. 1/2
5. 1/4
6. 1/2
7. 7/8
8. 1 1/4
9. 1 1/7
10. 1

WEDNESDAY
1. 1/3
2. 1 1/2
3. 8 1/2
4. 1/2
5. 4 1/2
6. 11
7. 7
8. 3
9. 5
10. 10

THURSDAY
1. T
2. F
3. T
4. F
5. F
6. F
7. F
8. F
9. T
10. T

FRIDAY
1. 4 in.
2. 10 cm.
3. 25 cm.
4. 12 in.
5. 15 cm.
6. 8
7. 5
8. 6
9. 0
10. 2

WEEK 40

MONDAY
1. T
2. F
3. F
4. T
5. T
6. T
7. T
8. F
9. F
10. T

TUESDAY
1. 1 1/4
2. 2
3. 3 1/4
4. 3/4
5. 3/2
6. 1/2
7. 2
8. 1 1/4
9. 1 2/5
10. 2

WEDNESDAY
1. 1 1/3
2. 5 1/2
3. 2 1/2
4. 10 1/2
5. 6 1/2
6. 11
7. 7
8. 22
9. 25
10. 31

THURSDAY
1. T
2. T
3. F
4. F
5. F
6. F
7. T
8. T
9. T
10. F

FRIDAY
1. 3
2. 4 in.
3. yes
4. 48 in.
5. 90 cm.
6. octagon
7. pentagon
8. hexagon
9. none
10. 1/2

WEEK 41	WEEK 42	WEEK 43	WEEK 44
MONDAY	**MONDAY**	**MONDAY**	**MONDAY**
1. 53,200	1. T	1. 7 & 5	1. 3 x 3 x 3
2. 345,000	2. T	2. 600	2. 60,000
3. 500	3. F	3. 6	3. 80
4. 44	4. T	4. 30	4. 8
5. 7,500,000	5. T	5. 81	5. 3,028
6. 750,000	6. T	6. 2,604	6. 125
7. 500.000	7. T	7. 300	7. 1,000
8. 7	8. T	8. 11/3	8. 2 1/3
9. 1,000,000	9. T	9. 1/10	9. 8 9/10
10. 1,000	10. F	10. $10	10. $1,000
TUESDAY	**TUESDAY**	**TUESDAY**	**TUESDAY**
1. 9/4	1. .9	1. 15	1. 20
2. 10/3	2. .09	2. 20	2. 25
3. 21/2	3. 9	3. 9	3. 8
4. 2 1/4	4. 7 1/2	4. 33	4. 40
5. 1 5/10 or 1 1/2	5. 150	5. 25	5. 300
6. 25	6. 80¢	6. 20	6. 25
7. 25	7. 750 g.	7. 20	7. 20
8. 9 3/4	8. 500 ml.	8. 25	8. 20
9. 41	9. 15	9. 15	9. 250
10. 25	10. 8	10. 30	10. 100
WEDNESDAY	**WEDNESDAY**	**WEDNESDAY**	**WEDNESDAY**
1. T	1. .5	1. 1 1/4	1. 1 1/4
2. T	2. .333	2. 1	2. 1 4/10
3. T	3. .25	3. 5 1/2	3. 2
4. F	4. .20	4. 8 3/4	4. 1 1/2
5. T	5. .10	5. 5	5. 1/4
6. T	6. .4	6. 22	6. 4 1/3
7. T	7. .3	7. 51	7. 2 3/5
8. T	8. .75	8. 4	8. 3
9. T	9. .6	9. 13 1/5	9. 1/4
10. T	10. .666	10. 4 1/2	10. 10 1/3
THURSDAY	**THURSDAY**	**THURSDAY**	**THURSDAY**
1. 40 lbs.	1. 36	1. 900	1. 91
2. 90 lbs.	2. 64	2. 5	2. 3
3. 120 lbs	3. 25	3. 10	3. 6
4. 25 lbs.	4. 9	4. 20	4. 12
5. 57 in.	5. 16	5. 17	5. 1
6. 9 in.	6. 49	6. 1,100	6. 900
7. 180 in.	7. 81	7. 900	7. 100,000
8. 240 in.	8. 100	8. 2	8. 3
9. 1,000 lbs.	9. 200	9. 7	9. 60
10. 126 in.	10. 8	10. 7	10. 5
FRIDAY	**FRIDAY**	**FRIDAY**	**FRIDAY**
1. 500	1. $10	1. 12 in.	1. 3 in.
2. 25	2. 30 dimes	2. 15 in.	2. 10 ft.
3. 750	3. 10 half-dollars	3. 35 in.	3. 30 in.
4. 100	4. 5 quarters	4. 36 sq. in.	4. 15 sq. ft.
5. 300	5. $100 bill	5. 150 sq. ft.	5. 34 m.
6. 45	6. 3,000 lbs.	6. 6.28 in.	6. 70 sq. m.
7. 36	7. gallon	7. 9.42 in.	7. 15.70 in.
8. 90	8. a foot	8. 60 in.	8. 12.56 cm.
9. 500	9. 2 yards	9. 48 in.	9. 25 in.
10. 90	10. 3 hrs.	10. 49 cm.	10. 80 cm.

WEEK 45

MONDAY
1. 10
2. 20
3. 104
4. 1/4
5. 12
6. 7
7. 10
8. 20
9. 10,000
10. 10,000

TUESDAY
1. 3
2. 8
3. 4
4. 33
5. 15
6. 5/10
7. 9%
8. 1
9. 1.2
10. 9

WEDNESDAY
1. 1/2
2. 1/4
3. 2/10
4. 1/3
5. 1 1/5
6. 1 1/4
7. 1 1/10
8. 11/10
9. 3/8
10. 4 1/4

THURSDAY
1. T
2. T
3. T
4. T
5. T
6. F
7. T
8. T
9. T
10. T

FRIDAY
1. square
2. radius
3. right angle
4. circle
5. obtuse
6. acute
7. decagon
8. octagon
9. cube
10. sphere

WEEK 46

MONDAY
1. -4
2. -14
3. 2
4. -20
5. -24
6. 17
7. -4
8. 8
9. 63
10. -12

TUESDAY
1. 5
2. 35
3. 13
4. 54
5. 78
6. 101
7. 345
8. none
9. 7 1/2
10. 3.8, 3.9

WEDNESDAY
1. 6.5 cm.
2. 1 1/2 ft.
3. 2 1/2 days
4. 1/4
5. 7/8
6. 125%
7. 5/7
8. 150 cm.
9. 3
10. $25

THURSDAY
1. 10
2. 33
3. 4 x 21
4. 6 x 9
5. $125
6. 2 kgs.
7. 2 liters
8. May
9. 200 sec.
10. 3 days

FRIDAY
1. 5
2. 7
3. 6
4. 4
5. 9
6. 8
7. 3
8. 10
9. 11
10. 12

WEEK 47

MONDAY
1. 450
2. 5
3. 25¢
4. 8
5. none
6. 44, 45
7. 130
8. 150
9. 15
10. -14

TUESDAY
1. 6
2. 35
3. 38
4. 300
5. 400
6. $11
7. 1/2
8. 3/5
9. 27%
10. 8.7

WEDNESDAY
1. 1
2. 3
3. 5
4. 7
5. 9
6. 11
7. 20
8. 40
9. 60
10. 90

THURSDAY
1. 180^0
2. 90^0
3. 90^0
4. 90^0
5. 60^0
6. 90^0
7. 60^0
8. 150^0
9. 40^0
10. 120^0

FRIDAY
1. 8
2. 7
3. 6
4. 1
5. 0
6. 2 1/2
7. 1/2
8. 7.5
9. .1
10. 10

WEEK 48

MONDAY
1. 17
2. 14
3. 15
4. 15
5. none
6. 47
7. 2, 4
8. 10
9. 3
10. 5 1/2

TUESDAY
1. 122
2. 25
3. 200
4. 2
5. 20
6. 54
7. 750 ml.
8. 18 hrs.
9. 3.6 in.
10. 200 lbs.

WEDNESDAY
1. 10
2. 5
3. 20
4. 40
5. 0
6. 90
7. 290
8. 490
9. 1/2
10. 27 1/2

THURSDAY
1. 11
2. 7
3. 40
4. 500
5. 8
6. 15
7. 6
8. 50
9. 7,000
10. 4

FRIDAY
1. 12:1
2. 3:1
3. 60:1
4. 7:1
5. 365:1
6. 4:1
7. 20:1
8. 2,000:1
9. 26:1
10. 2:1

WEEK 49

MONDAY
1. 20
2. 15
3. 20
4. 22
5. +2
6. -24
7. -1
8. +3
9. +5
10. -55

TUESDAY
1. $225
2. $17.50
3. 22
4. 13,000 lbs.
5. 850 cm.
6. 5,280:1
7. 8:1
8. 500:1
9. 50:1
10. 26:1

WEDNESDAY
1. 16
2. -1
3. 10
4. 20
5. 1
6. 5
7. -1
8. 0
9. 30
10. 30

THURSDAY
1. F
2. F
3. F
4. F
5. T
6. F
7. T
8. T
9. F
10. F

FRIDAY
1. 320
2. 243
3. 64
4. 625
5. 34
6. 77,777
7. 1,001
8. 567
9. 208
10. 4,500,000

WEEK 50

MONDAY
1. 2 x 5
2. 3 x 7
3. 2 x 11
4. 2 x 2 x 2 x 3
5. 5 x 5
6. 3 x 3 x 3
7. 3 x 5 x 2
8. 3 x 11
9. 3 x 3 x 2 x 2
10. 2 x 2 x 2 x 5

TUESDAY
1. 3:1
2. 6:1
3. 20:1
4. 12:1
5. 30:1
6. 40:1
7. 90:1
8. 100:1
9. 400:1
10. 2,000:1

WEDNESDAY
1. 95
2. 101
3. -1
4. 5
5. 8
6. 200
7. 5/8
8. 45
9. 2.000
10. 3.5

THURSDAY
1. T
2. F
3. T
4. T
5. F
6. T
7. T
8. F
9. T
10. F

FRIDAY
1. 320
2. 96
3. 2 1/3
4. 1.2
5. 23
6. 7,000,007
7. 12,500
8. 565
9. 59
10. 21

Notes

_____
_____
_____
_____
_____
_____
_____
_____
_____
_____
_____
_____
_____
_____
_____
_____
_____
_____
_____
_____
_____
_____
_____
_____
_____